Preface

The work reported in this publication forms part of the final report on the Australian Water Resources Council Research Project 71/25, <u>Drilling and Development Problems in Unconsolidated Sediments</u>. Associated work on the project, dealing with drilling mud invasion of unconsolidated aquifer materials, is reported separately in Australian Water Resources Council Technical Paper No. 17.

The research was carried out at the Water Research Laboratory of the University of New South Wales under the direction of the Project Leader, Mr. C. R. Dudgeon.

The assistance of members of staff of the Water Research Laboratory is gratefully acknowledged. The authors also wish to express their gratitude to members of the project reference panel for practical guidance during the course of the project. Membership of the panel was as follows:-

Mr. W. H. Williamson (Chairman) - Water Conservation and Irrigation Commission, New South Wales.

Mr. W. B. Lane - Irrigation and Water Supply Commission, Queensland.

Mr. A. A. Webster - State Rivers and Water Supply Commission, Victoria.

Mr. R. R. Hancock - Department of Mines, South Australia.

Mr. D. L. Rowston - Geological Survey, Western Australia.

Mr. H. F. Eggington - Water Resources Branch, Department of Northern Australia.

Dr. J. Gordon-Smith, Department of Environment, Housing and Community Development, Canberra, acted as secretary to the reference panel.

DEPARTMENT OF NATIONAL RESOURCES
AUSTRALIAN WATER RESOURCES COUNCIL

RESEARCH PROJECT No. 71/25

EFFECTS OF NEAR-WELL PERMEABILITY VARIATION ON WELL PERFORMANCE

by
C.R. Dudgeon
and
P.S. Huyakorn
Water Research Laboratory
University of New South Wales

AUSTRALIAN WATER RESOURCES COUNCIL
TECHNICAL PAPER No. 18

AUSTRALIAN GOVERNMENT PUBLISHING SERVICE
CANBERRA 1976

Published for the Department of National Resources on behalf of the Australian Water Resources Council by the Australian Government Publishing Service.

ISBN 0 642 50143 2

Printed by Canberra Reprographic Printers

Table of Contents

Page No.

1. Introduction   9.

2. Scope of Theoretical Investigation   10.

3. Steady Flow with Permeability Reduction in the
   Affected Zone   11.
   3.1 Theoretical Background   11.
   3.2 Mesh Calibration   13.
   3.3 Type Curves   14.

4. Transient Flow with Permeability Reduction in the
   Affected Zone   15.
   4.1 Theoretical Background   15.
   4.2 Fully Penetrating Wells   16.
   4.3 Partially Penetrating Wells   18.

5. Steady Flow with Permeability Improvement in the
   Affected Zone   18.
   5.1 Mesh Calibration   18.
   5.2 Type Curves   19.

6. Transient Flow with Permeability Improvement in
   the Affected Zone   20.

7. Proposed Method for Determining Aquifer
   Characteristics   20.

8. Conclusions   21.

List of References   23.

Appendix I: Tabulation of Results for Steady Flow with
            Permeability Reduction in the Inner Zone.   77.

Appendix II: Tabulation of Results for Transient Flow
             with Permeability Reduction in the Inner
             Zone.   95.

Appendix III: Tabulation of Results for Steady Flow with
              Permeability Improvement in the Inner
              Zone.   108.

Appendix IV: Tabulation of Results for Transient Flow
             with Permeability Improvement in the
             Inner Zone.   124.

List of Figures
(All Figures follow page 16)

Fig. No.   Title

1. Confined aquifer with affected zone around a fully penetrating well.

2. Confined aquifer with affected zone around a partially penetrating well.

3. Details of coarse and refined one-dimensional meshes calibrated.

4. Details of coarse two-dimensional mesh calibrated.

5. Details of refined two-dimensional mesh calibrated.

6. Plot of percentage errors in discharge for the one-dimensional meshes.

7. Plot of percentage errors in discharge for the two-dimensional meshes.

8. Details of specially discretised two-dimensional mesh.

9. Plot of percentage errors in discharge for the specially discretised two-dimensional mesh.

10. Type curves of Q/Q_o versus K_o/K_a (for l_{sc}/m = 0.2)

11. Type curves of Q/Q_o versus K_o/K_a (for l_{sc}/m = 0.4)

12. Type curves of Q/Q_o versus K_o/K_a (for l_{sc}/m = 0.6)

13. Type curves of Q/Q_o versus K_o/K_a (for l_{sc}/m = 0.8)

14. Type curves of Q/Q_o versus K_o/K_a (for l_{sc}/m = 1)

14a. Comparison of Q/Q_o versus K_o/K_a type curves for various penetration ratios.

15. Type curves of $\Delta w/2$ versus K_o/K_a (for l_{sc}/m = 0.2)

16. Type curves of $\Delta w/2$ versus K_o/K_a (for l_{sc}/m = 0.4)

17. Type curves of $\Delta w/2$ versus K_o/K_a (for l_{sc}/m = 0.6)

18. Type curves of $\Delta w/2$ versus K_o/K_a (for l_{sc}/m = 0.8)

19. Type curves of $\Delta w/2$ versus K_o/K_a (for l_{sc}/m = 1)

20. Type curves of $2\pi s_w T/Q$ versus $1/u_w$ (for l_{sc}/m = 1, r_a/r_w = 10, $10 \leq 1/u_w \leq 10^4$)

21. Type curves of $2\pi s_w T/Q$ versus $1/u_w$ (for l_{sc}/m = 1, r_a/r_w = 10, $10^4 \leq 1/u_w \leq 10^7$)

22. Type curves of $Q/2\pi s_w T$ versus $1/4u_w$ (for l_{sc}/m = 1, r_a/r_w = 2, $10 \leq 1/4u_w \leq 10^4$)

23. Type curves of $Q/2\pi s_w T$ versus $1/4u_w$ (for l_{sc}/m=1, r_a/r_w = 2, $10^4 \leq 1/4u_w \leq 10^7$)

List of Figures (cont'd.)

Fig. No.	Title
24.	Type curves of $Q/2\pi s_w T$ versus $1/4u_w$ (for $l_{sc}/m = 1$; $r_a/r_w = 4$, $10 \leq 1/4u_w \leq 10^4$)
25.	Type curves of $Q/2\pi s_w T$ versus $1/4u_w$ (for $l_{sc}/m = 1$, $r_a/r_w = 4$, $10^4 \leq 1/4u_w \leq 10^7$)
26.	Type curves of $Q/2\pi s_w T$ versus $1/4 u_w$ (for $l_{sc}/m = 1$, $r_a/r_w = 10$, $10 \leq 1/4u_w \leq 10^4$)
27.	Type curves of $Q/2\pi s_w T$ versus $1/4u_w$ (for $l_{sc}/m = 1$; $r_a/r_w = 10$; $10^4 \leq 1/4u_w \leq 10^7$)
28.	Comparison of transient and steady state type curves of Q/Q_o versus K_o/K_a (for $l_{sc}/m = 1$, $r_a/r_w = 2$)
29.	Comparison of transient and steady state type curves of Q/Q_o versus K_o/K_a (for $l_{sc}/m = 1$, $r_a/r_w = 4$)
30.	Comparison of transient and steady flow type curves of Q/Q_o versus K_o/K_a (for $l_{sc}/m = 1$, $r_a/r_w = 10$)
31.	Type curves of $2\pi s_w T/Q$ versus $1/u_w$ (for $l_{sc}/m = 0.2$, $r_a/r_w = 10$)
32.	Type curves of $2\pi sT/Q$ versus r/m (transient flow, for $l_{sc}/m = 0.2$, $r_a/r_w = 10$, $1/u_w = 0.17 \times 10^6$)
33.	Type curves of $2\pi sT/Q$ versus r/m (steady flow, for $l_{sc}/m = 0.2$, $r_a/r_w = 10$)
34.	Plot of percentage errors in discharge for the one-dimensional meshes.
35.	Plot of percentage errors in discharge for the two-dimensional meshes
36.	Plot of percentage errors in discharge for the coarse two-dimensional mesh.
37.	Plot of percentage errors in discharge for the more refined two-dimensional mesh.
38.	Type curves of Q/Q_o versus K_o/K_a (for $l_{sc}/m = 0.2$)
39.	Type curves of Q/Q_o versus K_o/K_a (for $l_{sc}/m = 0.4$)
40.	Type curves of Q/Q_o versus K_o/K_a (for $l_{sc}/m = 0.6$)
41.	Type curves of Q/Q_o versus K_o/K_a (for $l_{sc}/m = 0.8$)
42.	Type curves of Q/Q_o versus K_o/K_a (for $l_{sc}/m = 1$)
43.	Comparison of Q/Q_o versus K_o/K_a type curves for various penetration ratios.
44.	Type curves of $\Delta w/2$ versus K_o/K_a (for $l_{sc}/m = 0.2$)
45.	Type curves of $\Delta w/2$ versus K_o/K_a (for $l_{sc}/m = 0.4$)

List of Figures (cont'd.)

Fig. No.	Title
46.	Type curves of $\Delta w/2$ versus K_o/K_a (for $l_{sc}/m = 0.6$)
47.	Type curves of $\Delta w/2$ versus K_o/K_a (for $l_{sc}/m = 0.8$)
48.	Type curves of $\Delta w/2$ versus K_o/K_a (for $l_{sc}/m = 1$)
49.	Type curves of $2\pi s_w T/Q$ versus $1/u_w$ (for $l_{sc}/m = 1$, $r_a/r_w = 10$)
50.	Type curves of $2\pi s_w T/Q$ versus $1/u_w$ (for $l_{sc}/m = 0.2$, $r_a/r_w = 10$)
51.	Type curves of $2\pi s T/Q$ versus r/m (transient flow, for $l_{sc}/m = 0.2$, $r_a/r_w = 10$, $1/u_w = 0.17 \times 10^6$)
52.	Type curves of $2\pi s T/Q$ versus r/m (steady flow, for $l_{sc}/m = 0.2$, $r_a/r_w = 10$)

1. Introduction

Field evidence has shown that the specific capacity of a pumped well can be greatly affected by permeability variations which occur in a zone immediately surrounding the well. For a prescribed value of discharge a well drawdown in excess of the theoretical value, based on the assumption of a homogeneous formation, often results from permeability reduction in this narrow zone. If the well is drilled by a rotary rig, the reduction is likely to be caused by invasion of drilling fluids into the formation to form a mud cake. Other causes of reduction could be compaction during cable tool drilling and a blockage due to migration of fines or encrustation. To increase the permeability of the affected zone, the mud cake or other type of blockage has to be removed by applying an appropriate well development or stimulation technique. Under favourable conditions, continued development of the well can lead to an increased value of the coefficient of permeability which may become greater than the average value for the outer portion of the formation. When this condition prevails, a case of permeability improvement is said to occur. Whether one is dealing with the case of permeability reduction or improvement, a knowledge of the average coefficient of permeability in the affected zone and the radial extent of this zone is essential for correct interpretation of the behaviour of the well when pumped, proper control of development and efficient well operation.

Theoretical analyses of confined flow to fully penetrating wells with permeability reduction have been presented in numerous papers in the petroleum literature (Van Everdingen, 1953; Hurst, 1960; Jones, 1962 and Russel, 1966.) Much consideration has also been given to the case of permeability improvement accomplished by using hydraulic fracturing methods (Crawford et al, 1954; Gladfelter, 1955; Van Poolen, 1958 and Craft and Hawkins, 1959.)

In these papers, the term 'skin effect' is used to refer to the additional well drawdown due to permeability reduction. Various methods for determining the skin effect from pumping or recovery data of the well are also proposed. Recently, a number of workers have dealt with a similar situation of groundwater flow towards wells which are screened in confined aquifers. Krizek et al (1965) and Karanjac (1973) presented the theory and numerical solutions for the case of steady flow with continuous permeability variation in the vicinity of a well. Stromberg (1969) and (1973) presented analytical solutions for transient flow at constant discharge. In his analysis, the same assumption of a step variation of permeability coefficient as that commonly employed in earlier works on petroleum flow is made.

The investigations reported to date have not attempted to deal with the effect of permeability reduction or improvement on the production capacity or drawdown of partially penetrating or partially screened wells. It can be expected that the effect is likely to be more pronounced than that on fully penetrating wells due to vertical flow components. Furthermore, the proposed methods for evaluating the skin effect are based on the simplifying assumption that the additonal head loss or skin effect is independent of time and thus can be obtained directly from the corresponding steady state solution. The theoretical justification of this assumption has not been fully established.

The purpose of the present work is to investigate the effect of permeability reduction and improvement on the production capacity and drawdown of fully and partially penetrating wells which are screened in a confined aquifer and to present a method for determining the average coefficient of permeability in the affected zone and the radial extent of this zone. Numerical solutions of several transient and steady flow cases were obtained using the finite element programmes already documented by Huyakorn and Dudgeon (1973). The transient solutions covered a range of time values which included early times at which the assumption that skin effect is a time-independent variable is invalid. The results are presented in graphical form which enables a parametric study of dimensionless relationships to be conducted readily. Detailed tabulation of these results are also given in the appendices.

2. Scope of Theoretical Investigation

The following cases of steady and transient flow in a confined aquifer were considered:

(i) Steady flow with permeability reduction in the affected zone.

(ii) Transient flow with permeability reduction in the affected zone.

(iii) Steady flow with permeability improvement in the affected zone.

(iv) Transient flow with permeability improvement in the affected zone.

In obtaining the numerical solutions, a number of common assumptions were made in the finite element models for transient and steady state Darcy flow. Detailed description of the models have been given by Huyakorn (1973). The confined aquifer was assumed to be originally homogeneous and isotropic. The inner zone, bounded by a radius r_a, was then disturbed and its permeability coefficient was changed to a new value K_a which differed from the value K_0 for the outer region. For convenience in performing the parametric study, the permeability ratio K_0/K_a and the dimensionless radius r_a/r_w were varied independently. Several values of r_a/r_w within the range of $1.1 \leqslant r_a/r_w \leqslant 30$ were selected. For each selected value of r_a/r_w which was held constant, the permeability ratio K_0/K_a was allowed to vary from 1 to 100 for the case of permeability reduction and from 0.01 to 1 for the case of permeability improvement. It is believed that the ranges of both parameters, r_a/r_w and K_0/K_a, considered should cover the range of variation which is likely to be encountered in practice. Numerical results were obtained using sufficiently refined meshes consisting of triangular elements for 5 selected well penetration ratios of 0.2, 0.4,

0.6, 0.8 and 1. Detailed mesh calibration is described in later sections. The results are presented in the form of families of dimensionless type curves for steady flow under the conditions of prescribed drawdown and prescribed discharge and transient flow under constant discharge. For transient flow under constant drawdown, only the results obtained for fully penetrating wells are presented.

On the basis of the results of the parametric study, a method was developed for determining the permeability ratio K_o/K_a and the values of K_o and K_a from pumping test data. The method is described in a later section. Once the value of K_o/K_a is known, the performance of the well or its response to stimulation treatment can be assessed.

3. Steady Flow with Permeability Reduction in the Affected Zone

3.1 Theoretical Background

(i) Fully Penetrating Wells

Consider a confined aquifer with a fully penetrating well as shown in Fig. 1. Originally when the aquifer is undisturbed, the well drawdown-discharge relationship is given by

$$s_{wo} = \frac{Q_o}{2\pi K_o m} \ln(r_o/r_w) \tag{1}$$

where K_o is the undisturbed coefficient of permeability, s_{wo} is the drawdown in the well, Q_o is the discharge, m is the thickness of the aquifer, and r_w and r_o are the well radius and radius of influence respectively.

If the aquifer is disturbed such that the permeability in the inner zone, bounded by a radius r_a, is changed to K_a, it can be shown that the well drawdown-discharge relationship now takes the form

$$s_w = \frac{Q}{2\pi K_o m} \left[\ln(r_o/r_w) + (K_o/K_a - 1)\ln(r_a/r_w) \right] \tag{2}$$

For a well operating under the condition of prescribed drawdown $(s_w = s_{wo})$, the pumping performance may be assessed in terms of its productivity ratio which is given by

$$Q/Q_o = \frac{\ln(r_o/r_w)}{\ln(r_o/r_a) + \frac{K_o}{K_a}\ln(r_a/r_w)} \tag{3}$$

For a well operating under the condition of prescribed discharge $(Q = Q_o)$, the pumping performance may be assessed in terms of additional well drawdown (Δs_w) due to permeability reduction. Thus from equation (2)

$$s_W = s_{WO} + \Delta s_W \tag{4}$$

where

$$2 \pi K_o m \Delta s_W/Q = \left[(K_o/K_a - 1) \ln(r_a/r_w) \right] \tag{5}$$

Let the dimensionless well function be defined as

$$W = 4 \pi s_W K_o m/Q \tag{6}$$

Equation (5) may now be written as

$$\Delta W/2 = K_o/K_a-1)/n(r_a/r_w) \tag{7}$$

where $\Delta W/2$ is usually referred to in the petroleum literature as 'the skin effect'.

Equations (2), (3) and (7) are the exact analytical expressions which were used to check the accuracy of the finite element solutions obtained from various meshes. The results were subsequently used as a basis for selecting the meshes adopted to solve the partial penetration cases.

(ii) Partially Penetrating Wells

Consider a confined aquifer with a partially penetrating well as shown in Fig. 2. Since analytical solutions have not been developed for steady flow with permeability variation in the inner zone, it is necessary to express the productivity ratio and $\Delta W/2$ in functional form. On the basis of equations (3) and (7), Q/Q_o and $\Delta W/2$ for a partially penetrating well may be expressed as

$$Q/Q_o = f \left(\frac{K_o}{K_a}, \frac{r_a}{r_w}, \frac{r_o}{r_w}, \frac{l_{sc}}{m}, \frac{m}{r_w} \right) \tag{8}$$

and

$$\Delta W/2 = F \left(\frac{K_o}{K_a}, \frac{r_a}{r_w}, \frac{l_{sc}}{m}, \frac{m}{r_w} \right) \tag{9}$$

where l_{sc} is the penetration depth which is, in this case, also the length of screen and l_{sc}/m is the penetration ratio.

Equations (8) and (9) are the general expressions which are applicable to both partially and fully penetrating wells. The functions in these equations were evaluated using the finite element programs to obtain numerical solutions. Each solution led to one value of each of the two functions. Consequently, it was necessary to obtain a large number of solutions to cover the required ranges of values of the dimensionless parameters. Computational cost was thus a prime consideration in the selection of the two-dimensional meshes.

3.2 Mesh Calibration

(i) Fully Penetrating Case

In view of the high computational cost that may result from using an excessively refined mesh to obtain a large number of solutions, it was necessary to perform a mesh calibration and select the mesh which gives the required accuracy at a reasonable expense. For the case of flow to fully penetrating wells, two pairs of one-dinensional and two-dimensional meshes were calibrated. The one-dimensional meshes were included for a more complete study of convergence behaviour. Details of the automatic mesh generation may be obtained from Huyakorn and Dudgeon (1973). The one-dimensional meshes consisting of quadratic line elements are shown in Fig. 3. The length of the first line segment (FRLEN = Δr_1) was specified as 9 ft. and the lengths of the remaining line segments were calculated from $\Delta r_i = 2 \times \Delta r_{i-1}$ until the external radius r_0 was reached. The two-dimensional meshes consisting of triangular elements are depicted in Figs. 4 and 5, where FRLEN is the length of the first vertical block and THGP is the thickness of the affected zone. The values of FRLEN for meshes 1 and 2 are 1.89 and 0.43 ft. respectively. The lengths of the remaining blocks were calculated from $\Delta r_i = 1.5 \times \Delta r_{i-1}$ and $\Delta r_i \leq 200$ ft. to avoid ill-conditioned elements.

Solutions were obtained for several cases with different values of K_O/K_a but the same values of the remaining parameters in equation (8). For each case, the computed discharge was compared with the exact discharge given by equation (2). The results are plotted in Figs. 6 and 7, where ΔQ is the difference between the computed and exact discharges. Detailed tabulation of these results are given in Tables 1 and 2 of Appendix I. It can be seen that the coarser meshes give much less accurate results than the finer ones and that the accuracy obtained from all the meshes becomes poorer as K_O/K_a increases. The reduction in accuracy with increasing K_O/K_a is quite significant, particularly with the coarser meshes. Approximately the same degree of accuracy was achieved by using the finer one-dimensional and triangular meshes with a much greater number of nodes.

In the light of the above results, the procedure for selecting a proper mesh was reduced to a simple task of calculating $\Delta Q/Q$ at $K_O/K_a = 100$ and checking if its value was within the prescribed degree of accuracy. The finer one-dimensional and triangular meshes, which gave $\Delta Q/Q$ less than 3 per cent, were found suitable for subsequent use in obtaining a large number of solutions.

(ii) Partially Penetrating Cases

As analytical solutions to partial penetration flow with permeability reduction are not available, it was necessary to perform a convergence study prior to the mesh calibration to ensure that satisfactory convergence was obtained for the simulated flow situation.

The convergence study was accomplished by successively refining a particular two-dimensional mesh until the change in value of the computed discharge at K_O/K_a = 100 became negligible. It was found that for all penetration ratios less than 1, convergence difficulty was experienced when the depth of the affected zone was set equal to the length of the well screen. The convergence problem was caused by the base node on the screen, which contributed most of the total discharge at high values of K_O/K_a. In practice, this node would be blocked and its permeability reduced to the same value as that of other nodes on the screen. In view of this situation, the depth of the affected zone was slightly extended to a level below the screen base. To provide satisfactory discretisation of this zone for all values of its thickness (THGP), a general mesh shown in Fig. 8 was adopted. As illustrated, the aquifer was divided into two layers which were discretised separately. The mesh was successively refined and the convergence study repeated. It was found that satisfactory convergence was then achieved. Calibration was subsequently performed for 4 values of l_{sc}/m and r_a/r_w = 1.50. The discharge from a mesh similar to the one in Fig. 8 was compared with that from a more refined mesh with twice the number of nodes on the well screen. The results are tabulated in Table 5 of Appendix I and plotted in Fig. 9, where $Q_{mesh\ 3}$ denotes the discharge obtained from the more refined mesh. It can be seen that the percentage error in discharge is greater for smaller penetration ratios and that for each penetration ratio the error increases with increasing value of K_O/K_a. The maximum percentage error which occurs for l_{sc}/m = 0.2 is less than 6 per cent. This is satisfactory for practical purposes. The calibrated mesh was thus adopted for use in obtaining a large number of solutions.

3.3 Type Curves

After calibration and selection of the appropriate meshes, numerical solutions were obtained and the functions Q/Q_O and $\Delta W/2$ were evaluated for the selected values of their dimensionless parameters. Detailed tabulation of the mesh data and functional values are given in Tables 3, 4 and 6 of Appendix I. For a well operating under the condition of prescribed drawdown, the graphs of Q/Q_O versus K_O/K_a are presented in Figs. 10 to 14 for five selected penetration ratios. Each graph illustrates the effect of permeability reduction and the radius of the affected zone on the well discharge. It can be seen that the discharge ratio can be substantially reduced by serious permeability reduction (indicated by large values of K_O/K_a) which only needs to be restricted to a narrow zone of small r_a/r_w value. Slight permeability reduction in a zone of greater r_a/r_w value can also lower the discharge ratio significantly. On comparing Figs. 10 through 14 with one another, it is evident that the type curves in a family with a particular value of l_{sc}/m lie below 'the corresponding type curves with a greater value of l_{sc}/m. This evidence is shown more clearly in Fig. 14a. As indicated, the effect of permeability reduction on the discharge becomes more pronounced when the well penetration ratio is decreased.

In practice the type curves in Figs. 10 to 14 can be used to provide a quick estimate of the discharge Q if the permeability values K_o and K_a are known and in addition some estimate can be made as to the radial extent of the affected zone. With the parameters l_{sc}/m and r_o/r_w known from the geometry of the well and the aquifer, the value of Q/Q_o can be read from the appropriate type curve. The discharge Q_o from a homogeneous and isotropic aquifer may be calculated by using the following equation

$$s_{wo} = \frac{Q_o}{2\pi K_o m} \left[\ln r_o/r_w + \Delta \frac{W_p}{2} \right] \tag{10}$$

where $\Delta W_p/2$ denotes the additional dimensionless well drawdown due to partial penetration. It should be noted that $\Delta W_p/2 = 0$ for a fully penetrating well. In general, $\Delta W_p/2$ is a function of the dimensionless parameters l_{sc}/m and m/r_w. The function has been evaluated by Brons and Mating (1961) for selected values of these parameters. Type curves of $\Delta W_p/2$ versus l_{sc}/m have also been presented by Sternberg (1973). Knowing Q_o and Q/Q_o the discharge may be determined.

The graphs of $\Delta W/2$ versus K_o/K_a are also presented in Figs. 15 to 19 for a well operating under prescribed discharge. It can be seen that the skin effect increases rapidly with the increasing degree of permeability reduction. Each type curve shows a steep gradient at lower values of the permeability ratio and becomes approximately a 45 degree straight line as K_o/K_a increases to a value greater than 10. The vertical spacing of the curves appears to be approximately the same for different values of the penetration ratio.

In practice, the graphs of $\Delta W/2$ versus K_o/K_a can be used to determine the total well drawdown provided information is available on the values of K_o and K_a and the radial extent of the affected zone. For a specified geometry of the well and the aquifer the theoretical drawdown s_{wo} is given by equation (10). The value of $\Delta W/2$ can be obtained from the appropriate graph. Using this value the additional drawdown due to permeability reduction and the total drawdown are given by -

$$\Delta s_w = \frac{Q_o}{2\pi K_o m} \left(\frac{\Delta W}{2} \right) \tag{11}$$

$$s_w = s_{wo} + \Delta s_w \tag{12}$$

4. Transient Flow with Permeability Reduction in the Affected Zone

4.1 Theoretical Background

For a fully penetrating well which is pumped at constant discharge, a number of approximate analytical expressions have been presented for the well drawdown (Carter, 1966; Odeh, 1969; Sternberg, 1973). The expression most commonly employed may be written as

$$s_w = \frac{Q}{4\pi T}\left[\frac{\ln 2.25\, Tt}{r_w^2\, S}\right] + \frac{Q}{2\pi T}\frac{\Delta W}{2} \qquad (13)$$

where T and s are the coefficients of transmissivity and storage for the outer region of the aquifer respectively, and $\Delta W/2$ is the skin effect which is given by equation (7).

Equation (13) is based on the simplifying assumption that the skin effect is independent of time. The time range of validity of this assumption has not been fully established. However, the equation should not be used when the dimensionless time $1/u_w = 4\, Tt/r_w^2 s$ is less than 100 as the first term on the right hand side ceases to provide a good approximation of the exponential well function.

On the basis of the same assumption, equation (13) can be modified to predict the drawdown in a partially penetrating well. The modified equation may be written as

$$s_w = \frac{Q}{4\pi T}\left[\frac{\ln 2.25\, Tt}{r_w^2\, S}\right] + \frac{Q}{2\pi T}\left[\frac{\Delta W_p}{2} + \frac{\Delta W}{2}\right] \qquad (14)$$

where the values of $\Delta W_p/2$ and $\Delta W/2$ may be obtained using the steady state type curves for the partially penetrating well as described previously.

It is also assumed in equation (14) that the additional drawdown due to partial penetration is independent of time. This assumption has been shown by Sternberg (1973) to be sufficiently accurate when $1/u_w$ is greater than 10^4.

For a well operating at constant drawdown, no analytical solution to transient flow under permeability variation has been presented. The conditions under which equation (3) can be used to provide an approximation of the discharge ratios of a fully penetrating well is discussed in the following section.

4.2 Fully Penetrating Wells

Numerical solutions were obtained using a number of one-dimensional meshes which were identical to mesh 2 in Fig. 3 but with an external radius r_o of 5000 ft. and different values of Δr_1. Both the conditions of constant discharge and constant drawdown were treated. As the aim was to investigate the pumping response during early and late times, an initial time step size, Δt_1, was chosen such that the corresponding dimensionless time value $(1/u_w)$ was 0.10. The remaining time steps were automatically generated from $\Delta t_i = 1.41 \times \Delta t_{i-1}$ until the final time was reached.

For a well operating under constant discharge, the type curves of time-drawdown are plotted in Figs. 20 and 21. Each curve corresponds to a specified value of K_O/K_a and a common value of $r_a/r_w = 10$. The curve for $K_O/K_a = 1$ is merely the Theis curve, which is linear on a semi-logarithmic scale when $1/u_w$ is greater than 100. At each value of $1/u_w$, the skin effect ($\Delta W/2$) for a given value of K_O/K_a is obtained directly by taking the difference of the values of $\Delta W/2$ read from the Theis curve and the corresponding type curve. Table 7 (Appendix II) lists the values of the dimensionless well function and the skin effect at selected values of $1/u_w$. It may be observed that the skin effect increases with time and becomes approximately constant when $1/u_w$ is greater than a certain limiting value. This limiting value was taken to be 10^4, where all the type curves in Figs. 20 and 21 become parallel to one another. At early times, when $1/u_w$ lies within the range of $10 \lesssim 1/u_w \lesssim 10^3$, the type curves for various values of K_O/K_a show markedly different gradients. The gradient becomes steeper as K_O/K_a increases. At later times, for $1/u_w \gg 10^4$, the value of the skin effect was found to be very close to the corresponding steady state value which was read from the graph presented in Fig. 19. A direct comparison of $\Delta W/2$ values at various times with the steady state value is also given in Table 7. It may be noted that for $1/u_w \gg 10^4$, the difference between the $\Delta W/2$ values obtained from the transient and the corresponding steady state solutions is less than 1 per cent. Thus, in principle, one is justified in using equation (13) to compute the total well drawdown when $1/u_w \gg 10^4$. In practice, the real time value which corresponds to $1/u_w = 10^4$ is usually less than the first few minutes of the pumping test.

For a well operating under constant drawdown, type curves of $Q/2\pi T s_w$ versus $1/4u_w$ are presented in Figs. 22 to 27 for three values of r_a/r_w. Values of $Q/2\pi T s_w$ are also tabulated in Tables 8 to 10. Since s_w is maintained constant throughout the pumping period, each type curve shows the variation of well discharge with time. The curve for $K_O/K_a = 1$ can also be obtained directly from the analytical solution which has been presented by Jacob and Lohman (1952) for the case of transient flow in a homogeneous and isotropic aquifer. At a given time value, the relationship between the discharge and permeability ratios can be determined by direct reading from the type curves within a particular family. As the aim was to check if equation (3), with an appropriate selection of r_O/r_w value, could be used to provide a steady state approximation of Q/Q_O, the relationships of Q/Q_O versus K_O/K_a were obtained for several values of pumping time and are compared in Figs. 28 to 30 with the corresponding steady state relationship. It may be noted that for the selected value of $r_O/r_w = 1000$, the equation gives absolute errors which are less than 4 per cent when the values of the dimensionless time are within the range of $0.5 \times 10^5 \lesssim 1/4u_w \lesssim 10^7$. For a particular value of K_O/K_a, the discharge ratio decreases with increasing value of $1/4u_w$. This evidence is also shown in Figs. 23, 25 and 27 where it may be observed that the vertical distance between the type curve for $K_O/K_a = 1$ and each of the remaining type curves decreases as $1/4u_w$ increases.

4.3 Partially Penetrating Wells

Numerical solutions were obtained using a two-dimensional mesh which was identical to mesh 2 in Fig. 5 but with an external radius r_o of 5000 ft. Only the condition of constant discharge was treated. The time steps were generated in the manner described previously. The numerical results for the partial penetration ratio of 0.2 are listed in Table 11 (Appendix II). The type curves of W/2 versus $1/u_W$ are plotted in Fig. 31. It can be seen that as in the case of a fully penetrating well pumping under constant discharge, the type curves show markedly different gradients when the dimensionless time is within the range of $10 \lessgtr 1/u_W \lessgtr 10^3$, and that for $1/u_W \gg 10^4$ all the type curves are merely parallel straight lines. The skin effect of a partially penetrating well can thus be taken to be approximately constant at a late time value corresponding to $1/u_W \gg 10^4$. When the skin effect becomes independent of time, it is apparent that the material in the affected zone ceases to have influence on the time variation of the well drawdown. Consequently, it can be expected that for $1/u_W \gg 10^4$ the additional head loss at any point within this zone should also be independent of time and should be approximately equal to the head loss obtaining from the corresponding steady state solution. Figs. 32 and 33 show the dimensionless plot of the drawdown at the top of the aquifer versus the radial distance for $1/u_W = 0.17 \times 10^6$, and the corresponding plot obtained from steady state solutions respectively. It may be noted that the vertical spread of the type curves which gives a direct measure of the additional drawdown, is approximately the same in both figures.

5. Steady Flow with Permeability Improvement in the Affected Zone

5.1 Mesh Calibration

For the case of flow to fully penetrating wells, the one-dimensional and triangular meshes shown in Figs. 3 to 5 were calibrated against the exact analytical solution given by equation (3). The results are tabulated in Tables 12 and 13 (Appendix III). Figs. 34 and 35 show the plots of the percentage error in discharge versus the permeability ratio. It may be noted that there is a considerable improvement in accuracy of the numerical solutions obtained from all the meshes as the value of K_O/K_a decreases from 1 to 0.1. Further decrease in K_O/K_a does not, however, lead to a significant gain in accuracy. In fact, the accuracy of the two triangular meshes becomes slightly poorer.

For the case of flow to partially penetrating wells, it was necessary to calibrate a given mesh by comparing its solutions with the corresponding solutions of a more refined mesh as no exact analytical solution was available. The coarser mesh in Fig. 4 was thus calibrated against the more refined mesh in Fig. 5, which was also calibrated against an even more refined mesh. The results obtained for 4 penetration ratios are tabulated in Tables 15 and 16. For each penetration ratio the depth of the affected zone was set equal to the penetration depth as in so doing no convergence difficulty was experienced.

The plots of the percentage difference in discharge versus the perm-eability ratio are shown in Figs. 36 and 37.   As in the case of a fully penetrating well, it may be noted that the accuracy of both meshes improves as the value of K_O/K_a decreases from 1 to 0.1 and that further decrease in K_O/K_a does not lead to a significant gain in acc-uracy.   It is also apparent that poorer accuracy can be achieved for a well of smaller penetration ratio.   This is to be expected as flow in the vicinity of the well takes place under steeper hydraulic gradients.

In the light of the above results, it is sufficient to perform mesh calibration at $K_O/K_a = 1$ when dealing with the situation of permeability improvement. The coarsest, mesh which gives the required accuracy at this value of K_O/K_a should be selected for use in obtaining a large number of solutions.   Mesh 2 (Fig. 5), which was used previously when dealing with the situation of permeability reduction, was again adopted although, in principle, a coarser mesh would probably be sat-isfactory to achieve the specified degree of accuracy.

5.2 Type Curves

Using the selected triangular mesh, several numerical solutions were obtained and the functions Q/Q_O and $\Delta W/2$ were evaluated at the selected values of their dimensionless parameters.   Detailed tabula-tion of the functional values are given in Tables 14 and 17 (Appendix III). For a well operating under prescribed drawdown, the graphs of Q/Q_O versus K_O/K_a are plotted in Figs. 38 to 42 for five selected penetration ratios.   Each graph illustrates the effect of permeability improvement and the radius of the affected zone on the well discharge.   It should be noted that for a given value of r_a/r_w, the discharge ratio increases with decreasing K_O/K_a but its rate of increase diminishes when K_O/K_a decreases below a certain limiting value.   Each type curve approaches a horizontal asymptotic at small values of $K_O/K_a \leqslant 0.01$, which indicates that there is an upper limit for the increased well discharge due to permeability improvement.   This limit corresponds to the discharge obtained by extending the well radius to the radius of the affected zone.   On comparing Figs. 38 to 42 with one another, it is evident that for specified values of r_a/r_w and K_O/K_a, the discharge ratio is greater for smaller values of l_{sc}/m.   This evidence is shown more clearly in Fig. 43.   As indicated, the effect of permeability im-provement on the well discharge is more pronounced in a well of smaller penetration ratio.

For a well operating under prescribed discharge, the graphs of $\Delta W/2$ versus K_O/K_a are plotted in Figs. 44 to 48.   The skin effect takes negative values as the well drawdown is reduced by permeability improvement.   For a given value of r_a/r_w, $\Delta W/2$ varies in a manner similar to the discharge ratio as K_O/K_a decreases.

6. Transient Flow with Permeability Improvement in the Affected Zone

Numerical solutions were obtained in the same manner as described previously for the situation of transient flow with permeability reduction. Only the condition of constant discharge was treated. The results are summarised in Tables 18 and 19 (Appendix IV) for fully and partially penetrating wells respectively. Values of W/2 are plotted in Figs. 49 and 50 against $1/u_w$. As can be seen, at early times, when $1/u_w$ lies within the range of $10 \leqslant 1/u_w \leqslant 10^3$, the type curves show flatter gradients for smaller values of K_o/K_a. At later times, when $1/u_w > 10^3$, the type curves become parallel straight lines. To check the time range of applicability of equations (13) and (1 4), the values of the skin effect at various times are also listed in Tables 18 and 19. These values are compared with the corresponding steady state values. It may be noted that when $1/u_w \leqslant 10^3$, the absolute value of the skin effect increases with time and that when $1/u_w > 10^3$ the differences between the steady state and transient values are less than 1 per cent for both fully and partially penetrating wells.

As a final check, for the partially penetrating well, the type curves of drawdown at the top of the aquifer versus radial distance are plotted in Figs. 51 and 52. The vertical spread between the type curves appear to be the same for transient flow at $1/u_w = 0.17 \times 10^6$ and for steady flow.

7. Proposed Method for Determining Aquifer Characteristics

In order to predict the effect of permeability reduction or improvement on the well performance, it is necessary to know the values of K_o, K_a and S_s, and the radial extent (r_a) of the affected zone. To determine all of these unknowns, an aquifer test should be performed under constant discharge conditions. The data obtained should include the drawdown-time relationships collected from the pumped well and from two observation wells, one of which should be located as close as possible to the pumped well. The other observation well should be located at a distant radius outside the affected zone. Both observation wells should just penetrate the top of the aquifer. From the drawdown-time data of the distant observation well, the coefficients K_o and S_s can be determined using one of the conventional type curve methods given by Walton (1970) for fully and partially penetrating wells. If the pumped well is a fully penetrating well, the Jacob straight line method may also be used. Knowing the values of K_o and S_s, a dimensionless semi-logarithmic plot of drawdown versus radius can be made for a late time value. If the close-in observation well lies inside the affected zone, it is possible to determine the radius r_a by superimposing the field data plot on the appropriate type curve of $2\pi sT/Q$ versus r/m for $K_o/K_a = 1$ (Figs. 32 and 51). The value of r_a is simply located at the intersection of the type curve and a line joining the two points corresponding to the pumped well and the close-in observation well. Knowing K_o, S_s and r_a, the value of K_a can be determined from the drawdown-time data collected at the pumped well. A dimensionless semi-logarithmic plot of well drawdown versus time is made and the plot is then superimposed on the appropriate family of type curves of $2 \pi s_w T/Q$ versus $1/u_w$. At a late time, the value of $\Delta W/2$ is evaluated and used, in conjunction with the known values of l_{sc}/m, m/r_w and r_a/r_w, to determine the permeability ratio from the appropriate family of type curves of $\Delta W/2$ versus K_O/K_a (Figs. 15 to 19 and Figs. 44 to 48). For the fully penetrating pumped well, it is probably more convenient to use equation (7) rather than the type curves. Knowing K_O and K_O/K_a, the value of K_a can be determined.

In a majority of practical cases where the radial extent of the affected zone is less than a few feet, it is not possible to construct an observation well inside this zone. Thus one has to rely solely on the drawdown-time data collected at the pumped well in determining K_a and r_a. It is apparent in Figs. 15 to 19 that the two unknowns K_a and r_a cannot be uniquely determined using only a given value of $\Delta W/2$. Consequently, it is necessary to estimate a probable value (or range of values) for one unknown and evaluate the corresponding value for the remaining unknown. For a situation of permeability reduction, where $\Delta W/2$ is positive, the value of r_a should be estimated and the corresponding value of K_a determined from the type curves noting that the term r_a/r_w appears in a logarithmic form in equation (7). For a situation of permeability improvement, where $\Delta W/2$ is negative, the value of K_a should be estimated as it can be seen from Figs. 44 to 48 that $\Delta W/2$ is not sensitive to K_O/K_a if it lies within the range of $0.01 \leq K_O/K_a \leq 0.1$. If there exists a close observation well and it happens to be outside the affected zone, the value of r_a determined should be smaller than the radius to this observation well.

Where possible, the drawdown at the pumped well should be measured during early pumping times when $1/u_w$ is smaller than 10^4 as it has been demonstrated that the shape of the type curves of $2 \pi s_w T/Q$ versus K_O/K_a depends on K_O/K_a. The early time-drawdown data may prove to be useful in providing an additional check on the determined values of K_a and r_a.

8. Conclusions

1. The effect of permeability variations on pumping performance of fully and partially penetrating wells in a confined aquifer has been investigated by using the finite element programs to solve a large number of transient and steady state, Darcy flow problems. Both the situations of permeability reduction and improvement have been treated.

2. For steady state flow, type curves of the discharge ratio versus permeability ratio and type curves of the skin effect versus permeability ratio have been presented. The type curves enable the well discharge and the total drawdown to be evaluated for a given value of the permeability ratio. It was found that the effect of a specified permeability reduction or improvement is more pronounced with decreasing well penetration ratio.

3.   For transient flow under constant discharge, type curves of the dimensionless well drawdown versus dimensionless time have been presented.   The type curves for different values of the permeability ratio show markedly different gradients for early time values which correspond to $10 \leq 1/u_w \leq 10^3$.   The gradient increases with increasing permeability ratio K_o/K_a.   The curves become parallel straight lines for $1/u_w \gg 10^4$.   A comparison was made between the values of the skin effect obtained from transient and corresponding steady state solutions.   It was found that when $1/u_w \gg 10^4$, the difference between the transient and steady state values is less than 1 per cent for fully and partially penetrating wells.

4.   For transient flow to a fully penetrating well operating under constant drawdown, type curves of the dimensionless well discharge versus dimensionless time have been presented.   From these curves, the transient relationships between the discharge ratio and the permeability ratio were obtained and compared with the corresponding steady state relationships obtained from an analytical equation using a selected value of $r_o/r_w = 1000$.   It was found that the equation gives absolute errors in the discharge ratio which are less than 4 per cent for $0.5 \times 10^5 \leq 1/4u_w \leq 10^7$.

5. A method has been proposed for determining from pumping tests the aquifer characteristics K_o, K_a, S_s and r_a.   It has been pointed out that to determine uniquely the values of K_a and r_a the field data must include the time-drawdown relationship collected from a close-in observation well which lies inside the affected zone.

6.   The results of this investigation are applicable only to wells affected by losses due to Darcy flow and do not account for losses due to non-Darcy flow that may occur near the well, particularly under the situation of permeability improvement.

List of References

1. Bixel, H.C. and Van Poolen, H.K. - "Pressure drawdown and build-up in presence of radial discontinuities", Soc. Pet. Eng. Jour., pp. 301-309, (1967).

2. Brons, F. and Marting, V.E. - "The effect of restricted fluid entry on well productivity", Jour. of Petroleum Technology, Vol. 13, No. 2, pp. 172-174, (1961).

3. Carter, R.D. - "Pressure behaviour of limited circular composite reservoir", Soc. Pet. Eng. Jour. pp. 328-334, (1966).

4. Craft, B.C. and Hawkins, M.F. - "Petroleum Reservoir Engineering", Prentice-Hall, Englewood Cliff, N.J., (1959).

5. Crawford, P.B. et al - "Estimated effect of horizontal fractures on production capacity", Paper 414-G presented at the AIME Meeting, San Antonio, Texas, Oct. (1954).

6. Demson, K.H. et al - "Permeability of sand with dispersed clay particles", Water Resources Research, Vol. 6, No. 4, pp. 1275-1276, (1968).

7. Gatlin, C. - "Petroleum Engineering - Drilling and Well Completions", Prentice-Hall, Englewood Cliffs, N.J., (1960).

8. Gladfelter, R.E. et al - "Selecting wells which will respond to production stimulation treatment", Drilling and Production Practice, pp. 117-129, (1955).

9. Hurst, W. -"Establishment of the skin effect and its impediment to thin flow into a well bore", The Petroleum Engineer, Vol. 25, No. 10, pp. B6-B16, (1953).

10. Huyakorn, P.S. -"Finite element solution of two-regime flow towards wells", Ph. D. Thesis, Uni. of New South Wales, 191 pp. Dec. (1973).

11. Huyakorn, P.S. and Dudgeon, C.R. - "Finite element computer programs for analysing flow towards wells", Uni. of New South Wales, Water Research Lab., Report No. 135, 316 pp. (1974).

12. Jacob, C.E. and Lohman, S.W. - "Nonsteady flow to a well of a constant drawdown in an extensive aquifer", Trans. Amer. Geophys. Union, Vol. 33, No. 4, (1952).

13. Jones, P. - "Permeability and radius of a skin", The Oil and Gas Jour., Vol. 60, No. 25, pp. 114-119, (1962).

14. Karanjac, J. - "Well losses due to reduced formation permeability", Ground Water, Vol. 10, No. 4, pp. 42-46, (1972).

List of References (cont'd.)

15. Krizek, R.J. et al - "Well capacity for continuous permeability variation", ASCE Jour. of Irr. Div., Vol. 95, No. IR3, pp. 409-414, (1969).

16. Odeh, A.S. - "Flow test analysis for a well with radial discontinuity", Soc. Pet. Eng. Jour., pp. 207-210, (1969).

17. Russel, D.G. - "Extension of pressure build-up analysis methods", Jour. of Petroleum Technology, Vol. 18, No. 12, pp. 1624-1636, (1966).

18. Sternberg, Y.M. - "Flow to wells in the presence of radial discontinuities", Ground Water, Vol. 7, No. 6, pp. 17-20, (1969).

19. Sternberg, Y.M. - "Theory and application of the skin effect concept to groundwater wells", Int. Symp. on Development of Ground Water Resources", Madras, India, Vol. 2, pp. 23-32, Nov. (1973).

20. Sternberg, Y.M. - "Efficiency of partially penetrating wells", Ground Water, Vol. 11, No. 3, pp. 5-8, (1973).

21. Van Everdingen, A.F. - "The skin effect and its influence on the productive capacity of a well", Trans. Amer. Inst. of Minn. and Metal Eng., Vol. 198, pp. 305-324, (1953).

22. Van Poolen, H.K. et al - "Hydraulic fracturing: Fracture flow capacity Vs. well productivity", Petroleum Trans., AIME, Vol. 213, pp. 91-95, (1958).

23. Walton, W.C. - "Groundwater Resource Evaluation", McGraw-Hill Book Co. (1970).

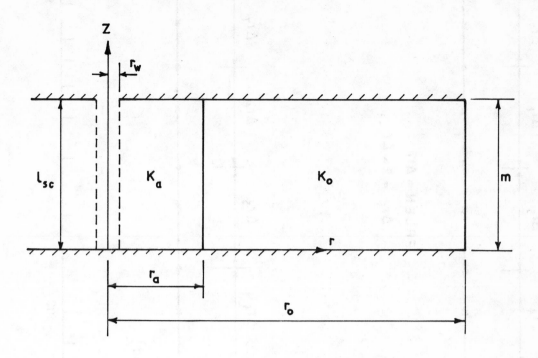

Figure 1:   Confined aquifer with affected zone around
a fully penetrating well.

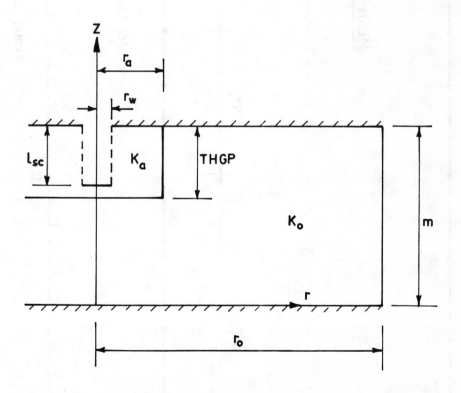

Figure 2:   Confined aquifer with affected zone around
a partially penetrating well.

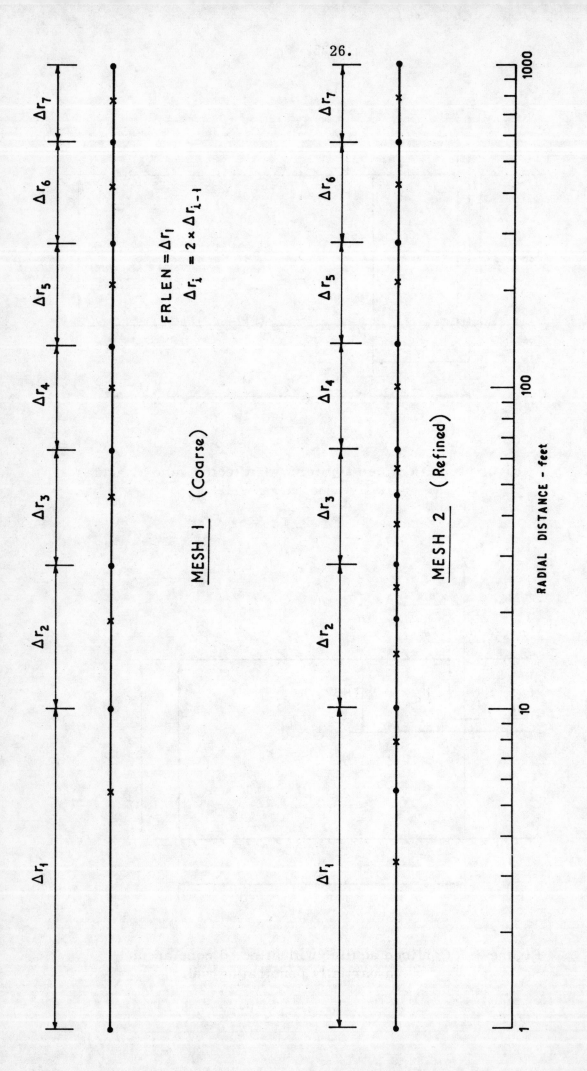

Figure 3: Details of coarse and refined one-dimensional meshes calibrated.

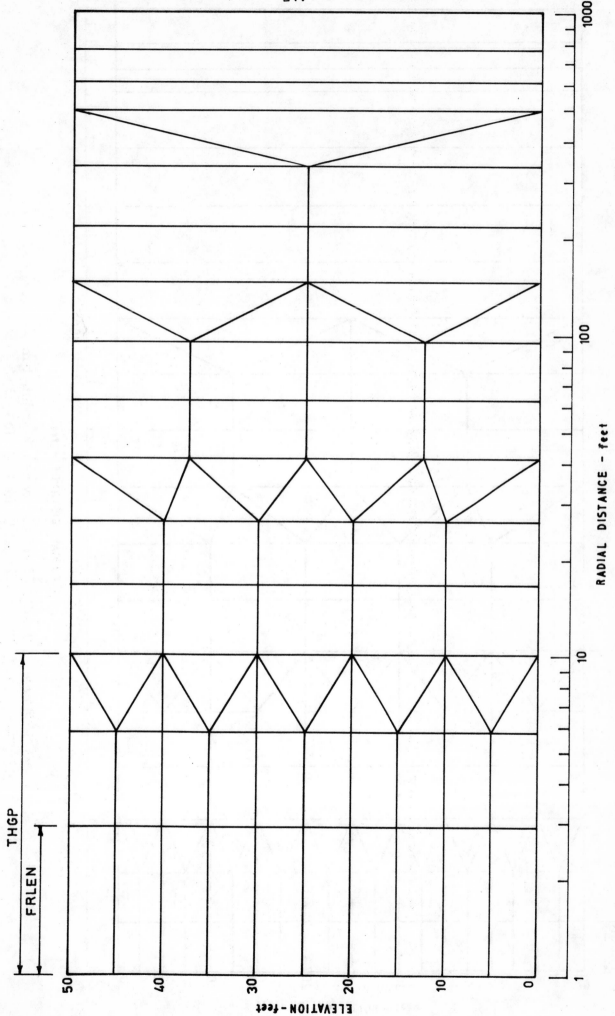

Figure 4: Details of coarse two-dimensional mesh calibrated. (Mesh 1)

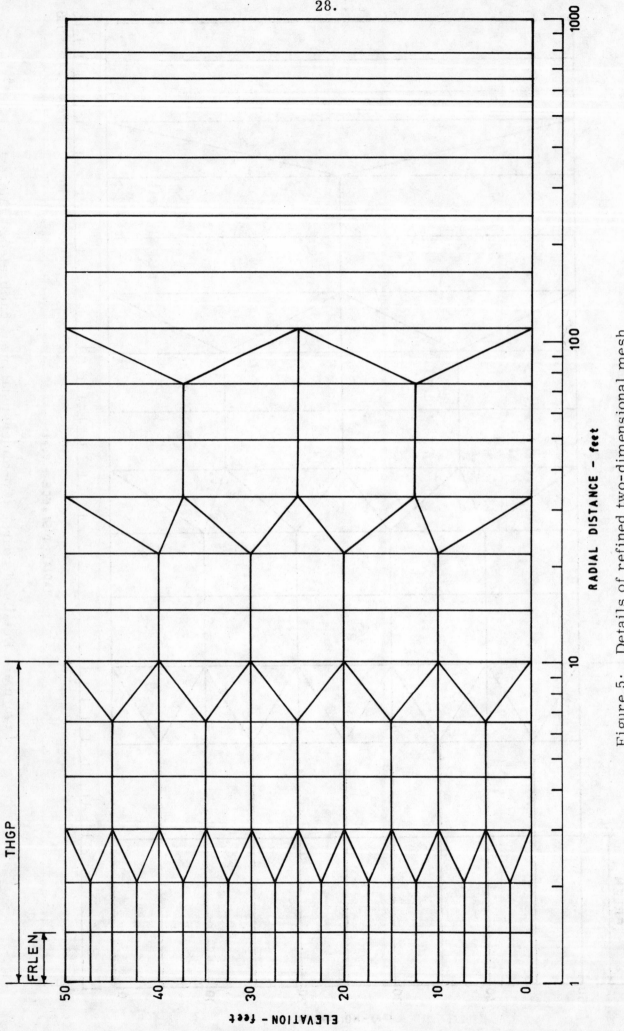

Figure 5: Details of refined two-dimensional mesh
calibrated. (Mesh 2)

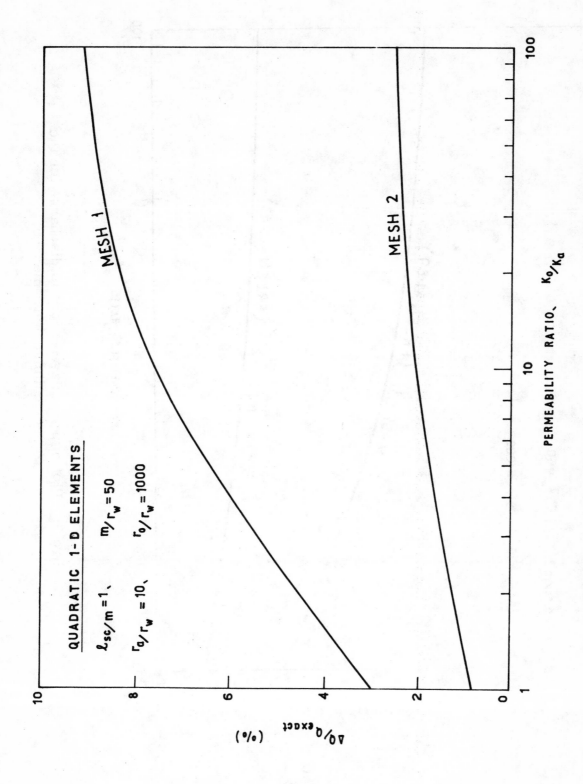

Figure 6: Plot of percentage errors in discharge for the one-dimensional meshes.

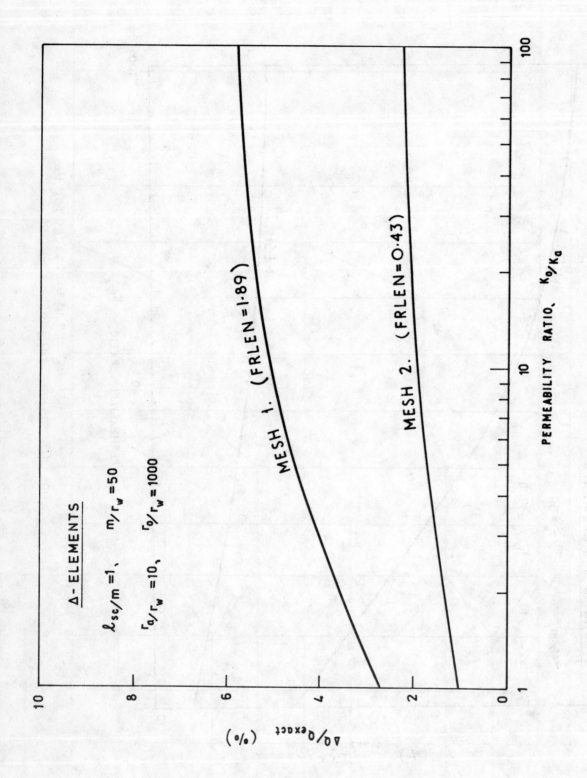

Figure 7: Plot of percentage errors in discharge for the two-dimensional meshes.

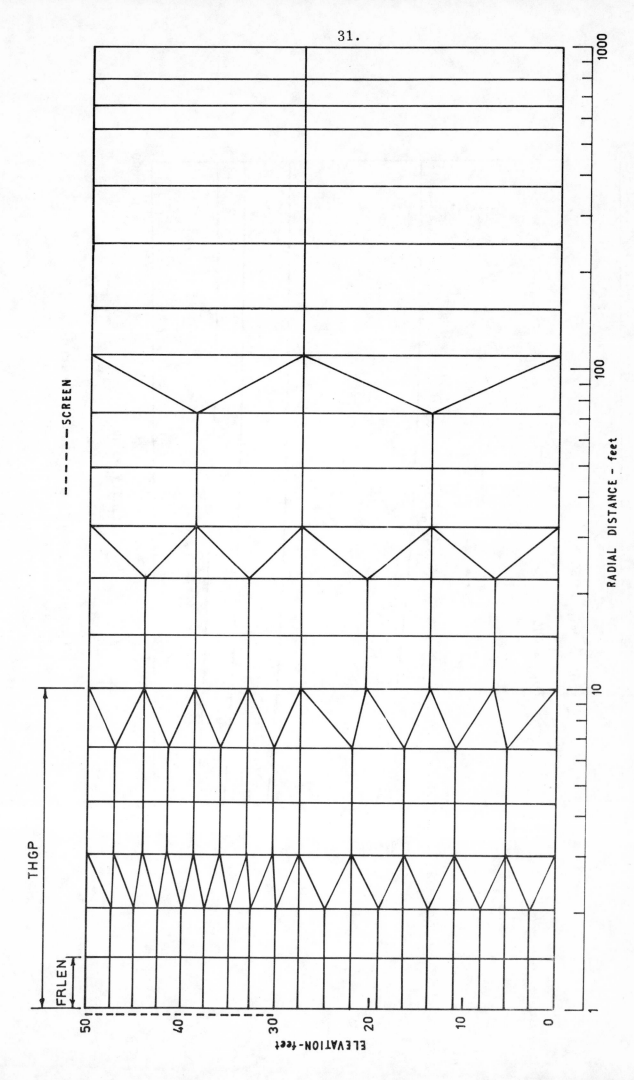

Figure 8: Details of specially discretised two-dimensional mesh. (Mesh 2a)

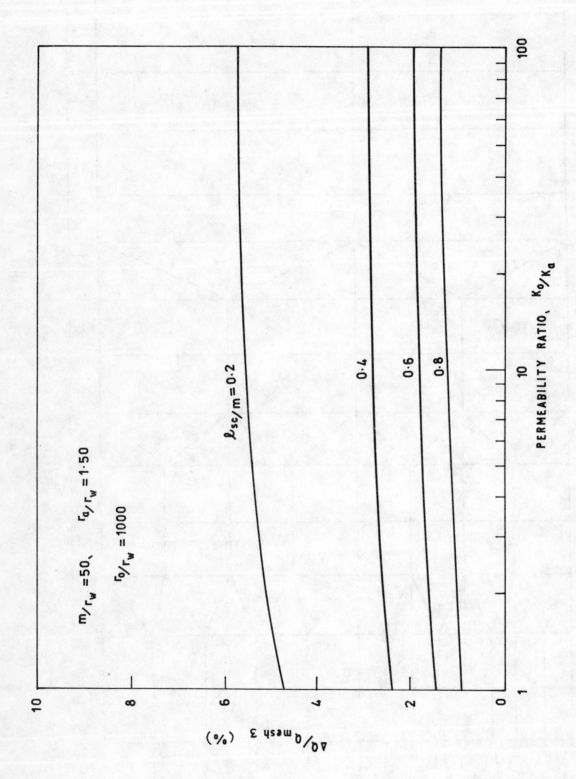

Figure 9: Plot of percentage errors in discharge for the specially discretised two-dimensional mesh.

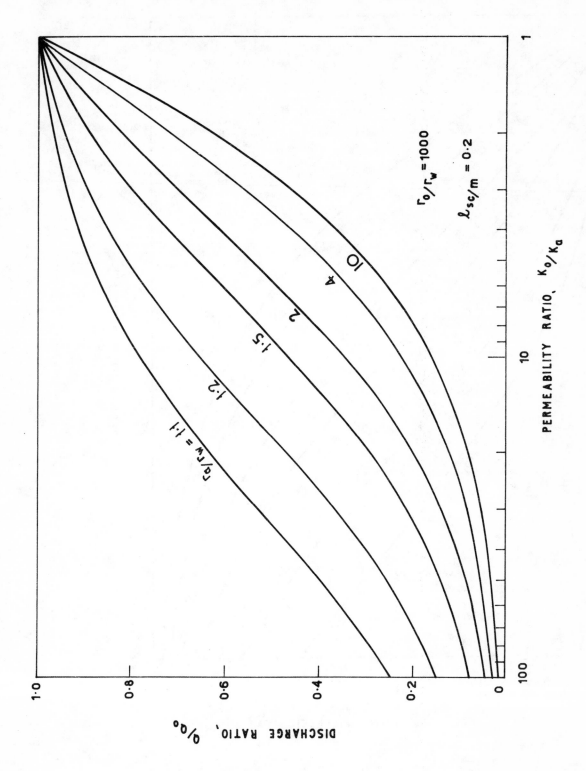

Figure 10:   Type curves of Q/Q_o versus K_o/K_a (for $l_{sc}/m = 0.2$)

34.

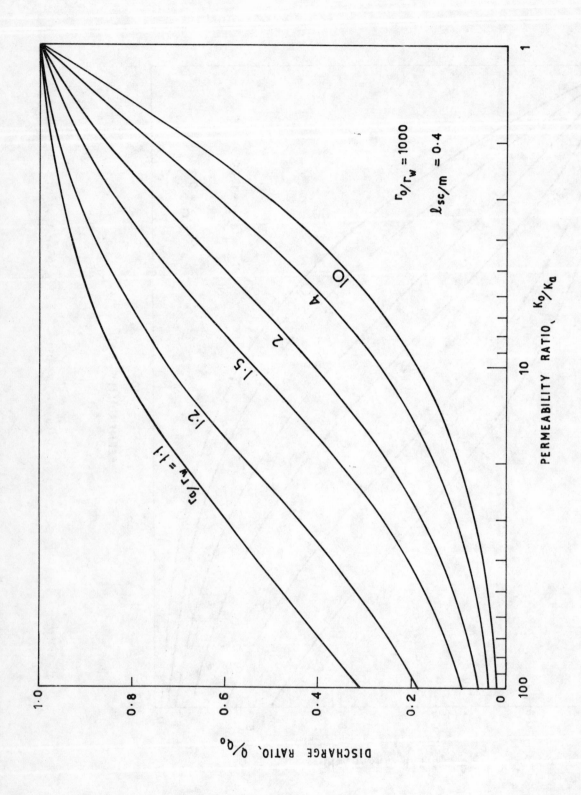

Figure 11: Type curves of Q/Q_o versus K_o/K_a
(for $l_{sc}/m = 0.4$)

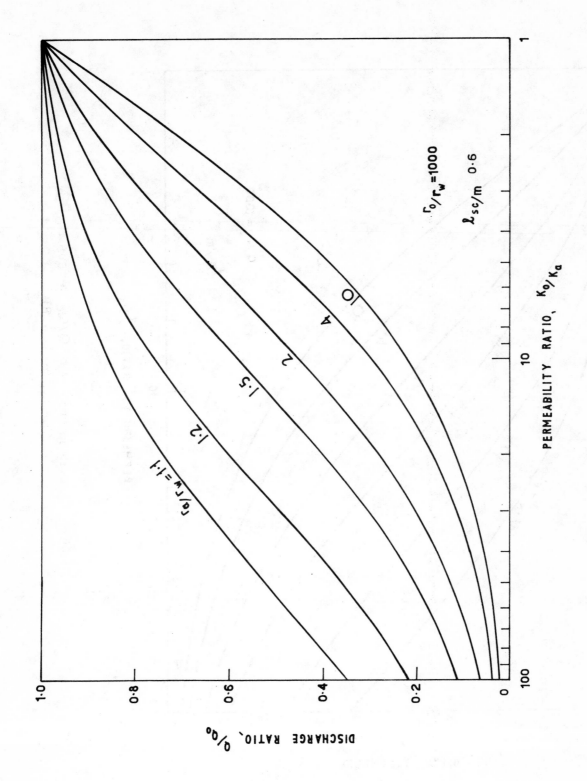

Figure 12:   Type curves of Q/Q_O versus K_O/K_a
(for l_{sc}/m = 0.6)

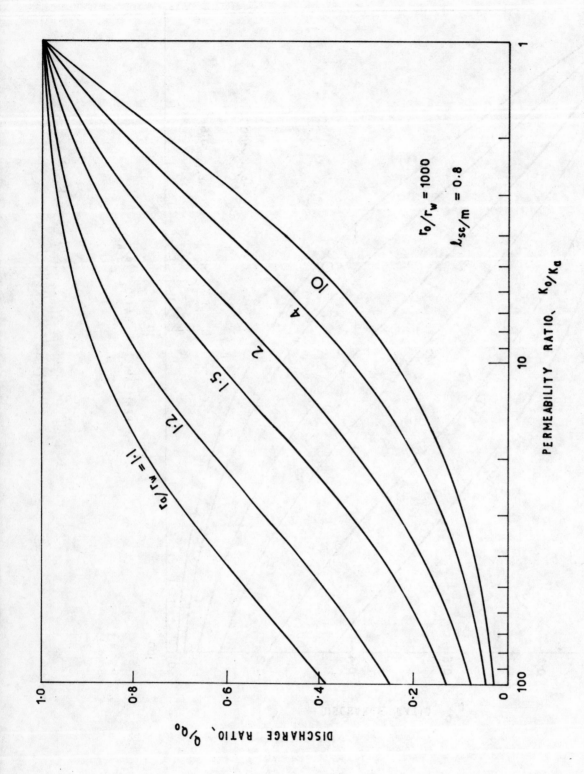

Figure 13: Type curves of Q/Q_o versus K_o/K_a
(for l_{sc}/m = 0.8)

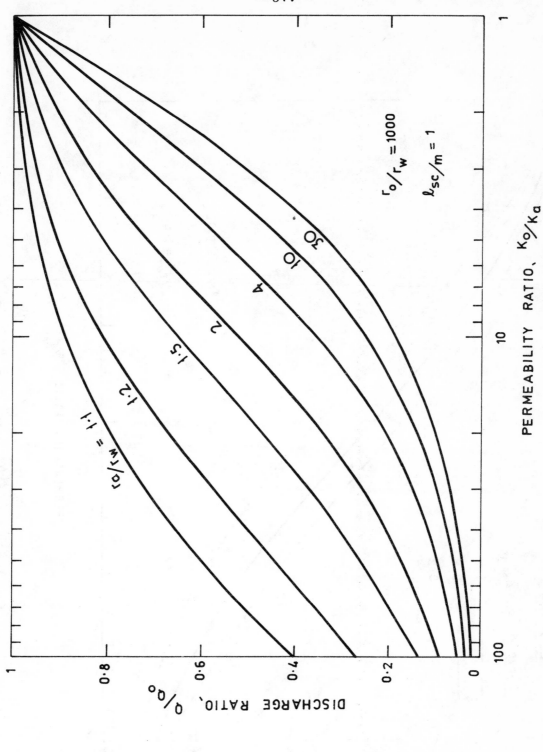

Figure 14: Type curves of Q/Q_o versus K_O/K_a
(for $l_{sc}/m = 1$)

38.

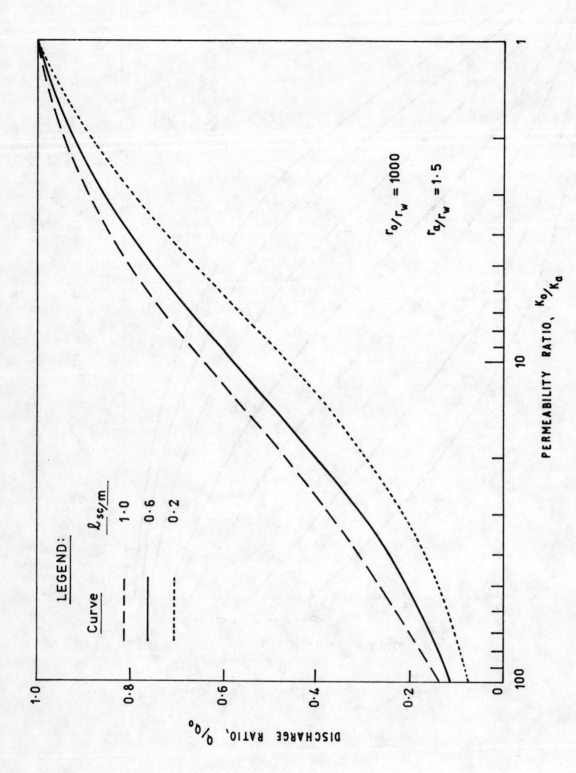

Figure 14a: Comparison of Q/Q_o versus K_o/K_a type curves for various penetration ratios.

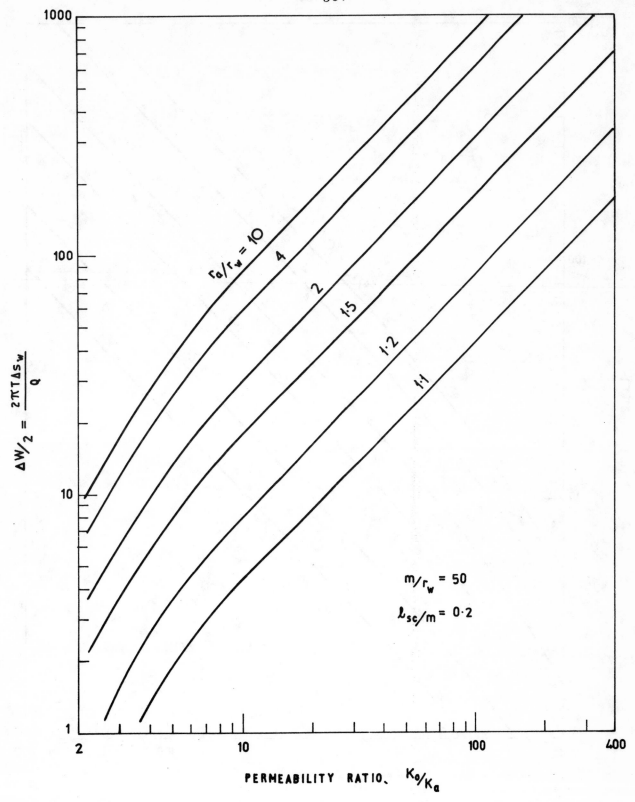

Figure 15: Type curves of $\Delta w/2$ versus K_O/K_a
(for $l_{sc}/m = 0.2$)

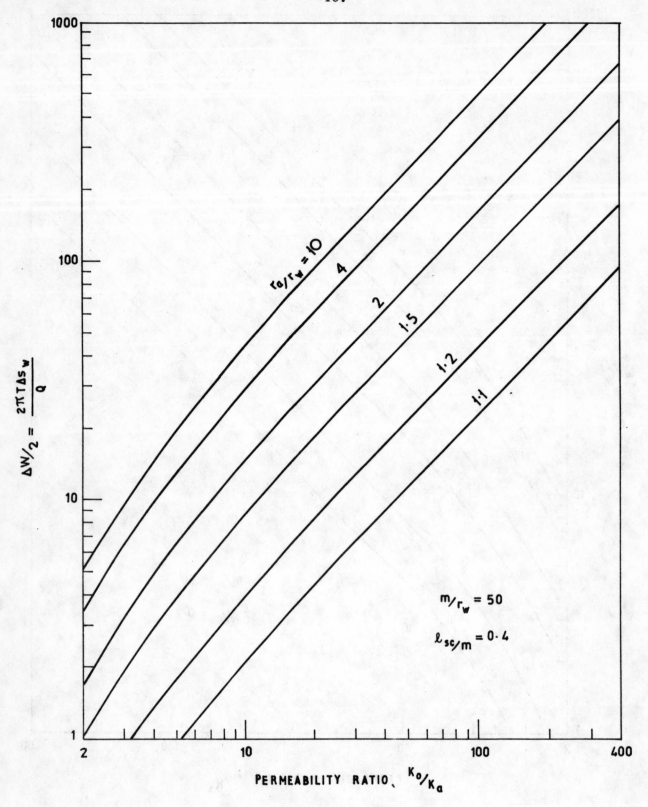

Figure 16: Type curves of $\Delta w/2$ versus K_o/K_a
(for l_{sc}/m = 0.4)

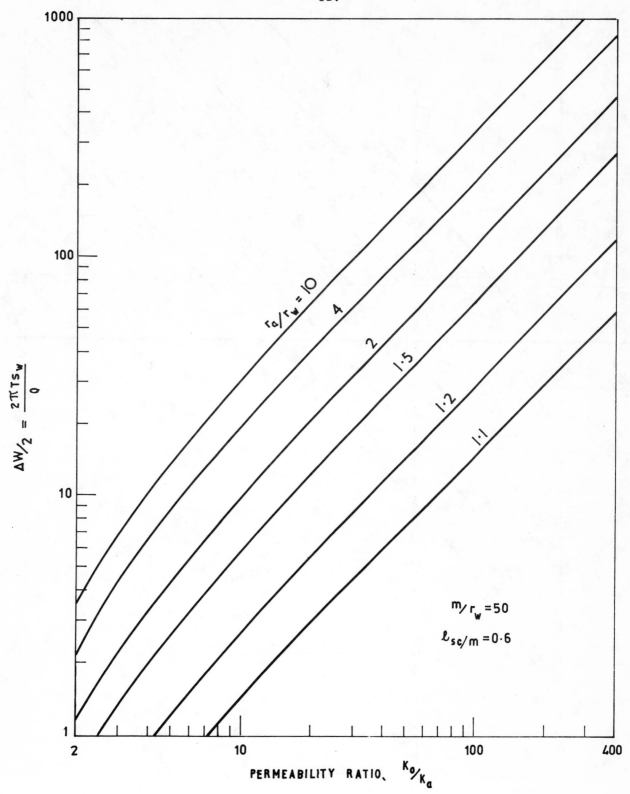

Figure 17:   Type curves of $\Delta w/2$ versus K_O/K_a
(for l_{sc}/m = 0.6)

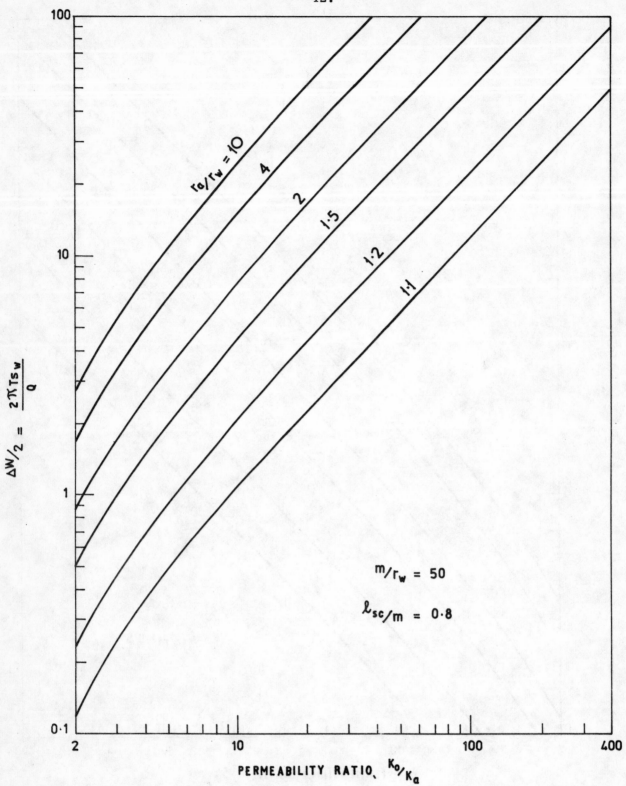

Figure 18: Type curves of $\Delta w/2$ versus K_O/K_a
(for $l_{sc}/m = 0.8$)

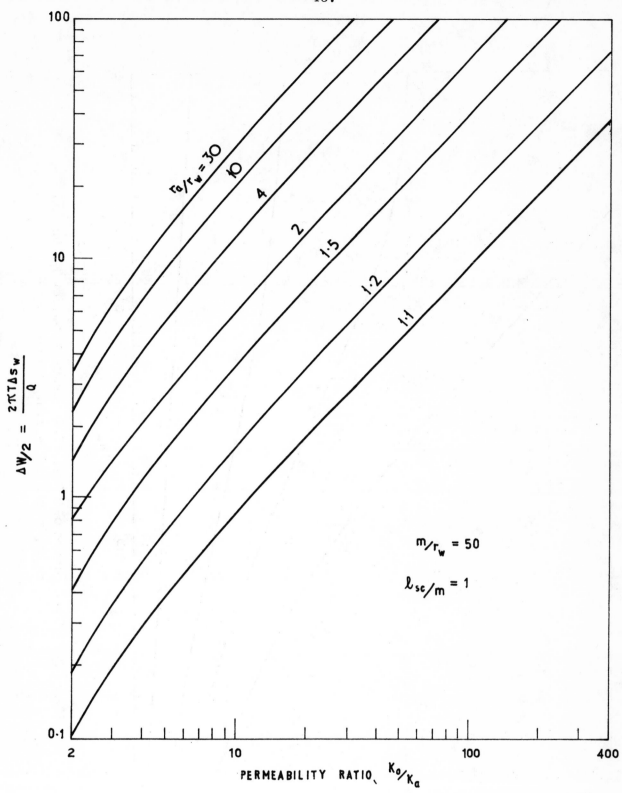

Figure 19:   Type curves of $\triangle w/2$ versus K_o/K_a
(for l_{sc}/m = 1)

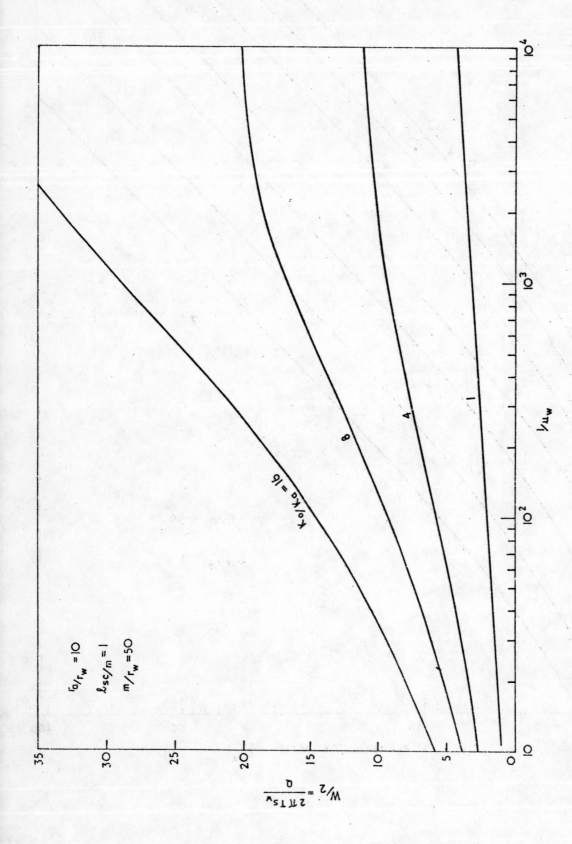

Figure 20: Type curves of $2\pi s_w T/Q$ versus $1/u_w$ (for $l_{sc}/m = 1$, $r_a/r_w = 10$, $10 \leq 1/u_w \leq 10^4$)

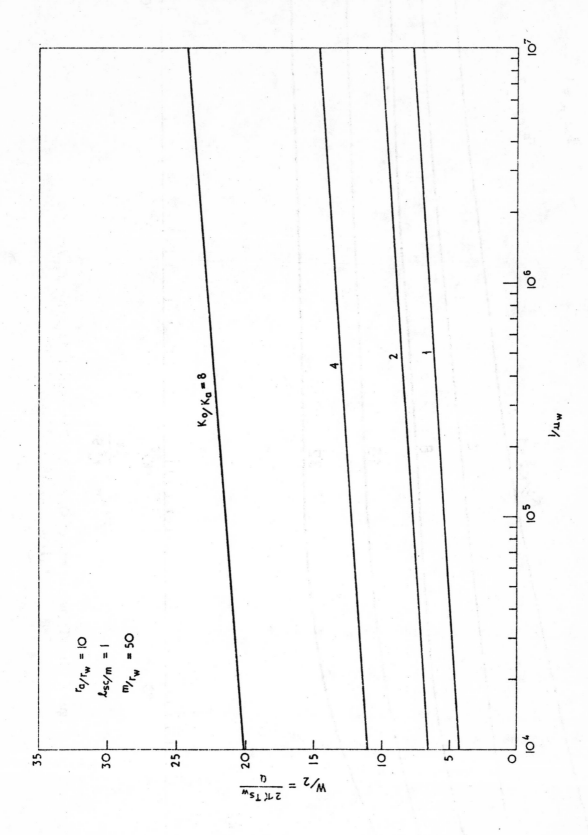

Figure 21: Type curves of $2\pi\,s_w\,T/Q$ versus $1/u_w$ (for $l_{sc}/m = 1$, $r_a/r_w = 10$, $10^4 \leqslant 1/u_w \leqslant 10^7$)

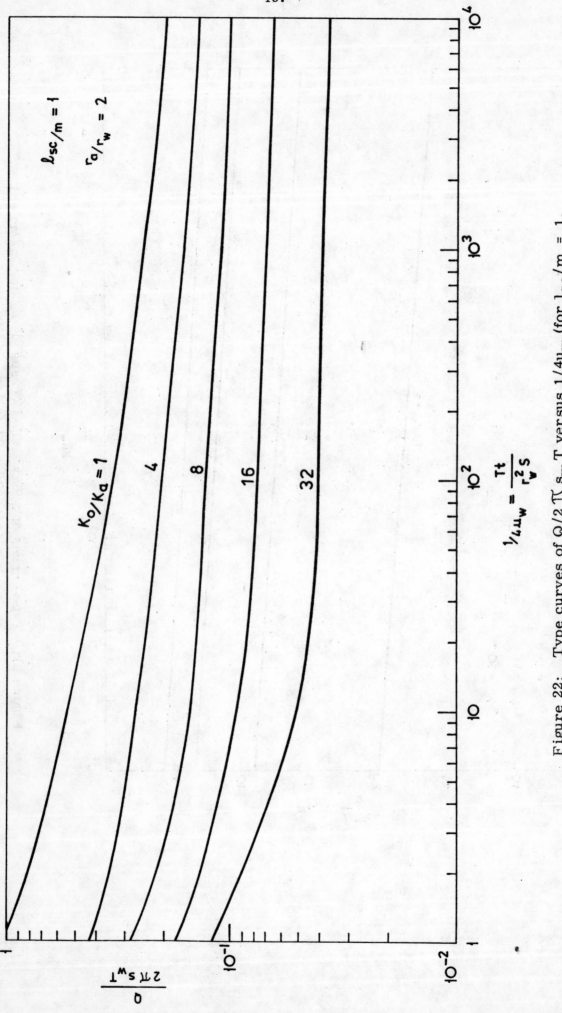

Figure 22: Type curves of $Q/2\pi s_w T$ versus $1/4u_w$ (for $l_{sc}/m = 1$, $r_a/r_w = 2$, $10 \leq 1/4u_w \leq 10^4$)

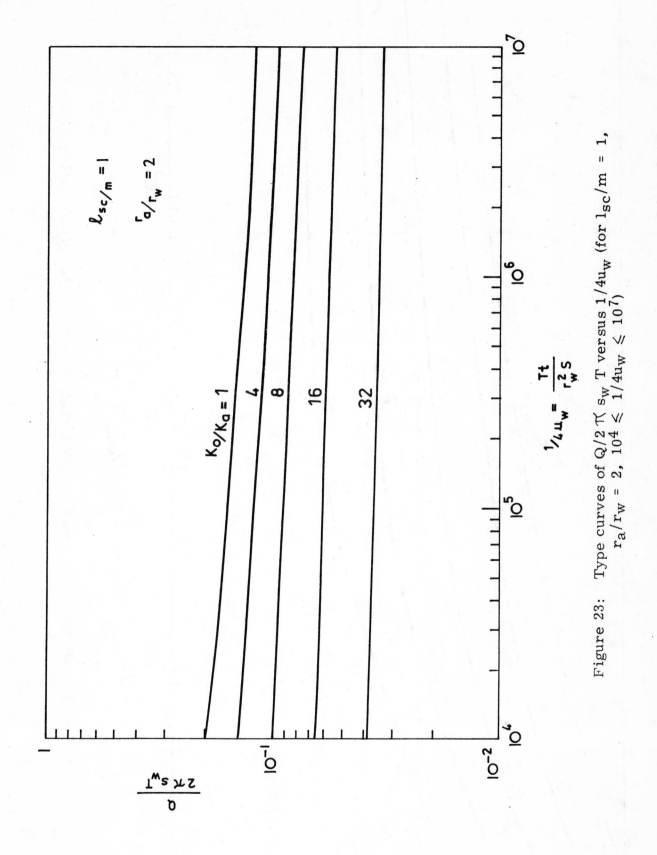

Figure 23: Type curves of $Q/2\pi s_w T$ versus $1/4u_w$ (for $l_{sc}/m = 1$, $r_a/r_w = 2$, $10^4 \leqslant 1/4u_w \leqslant 10^7$)

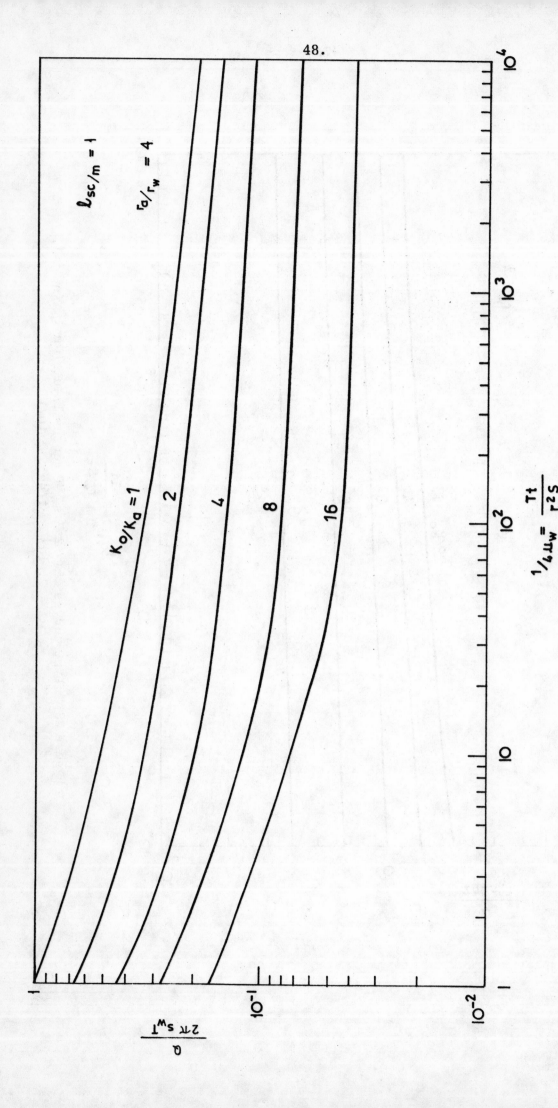

Figure 24: Type curves of $Q/2\pi\, s_w T$ versus $1/4u_w$ (for $l_{sc}/m = 1$, $r_a/r_w = 4$, $10 \leqslant 1/4u_w \leqslant 10^4$)

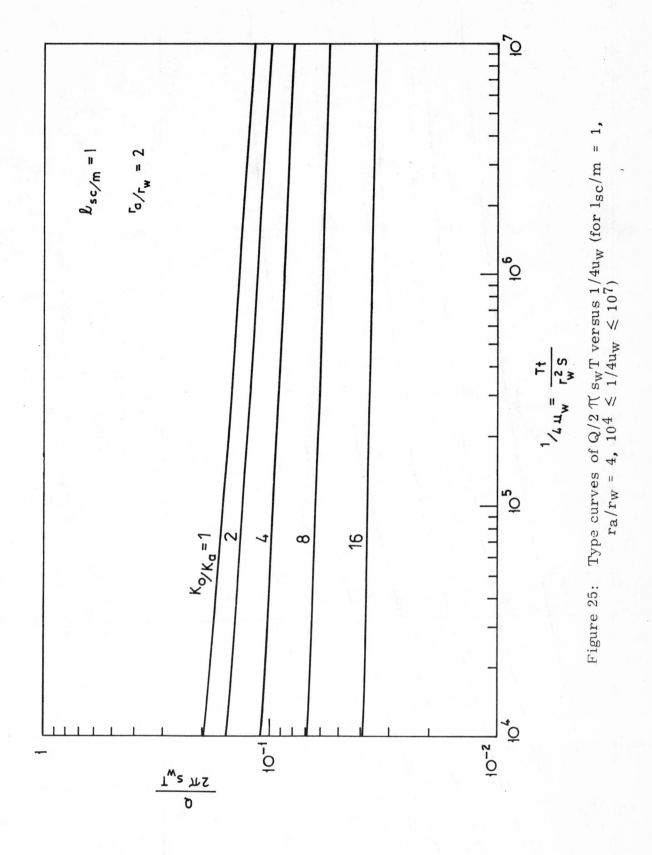

Figure 25: Type curves of $Q/2\pi s_w T$ versus $1/4u_w$ (for $l_{sc}/m = 1$, $r_a/r_w = 4$, $10^4 \leq 1/4u_w \leq 10^7$)

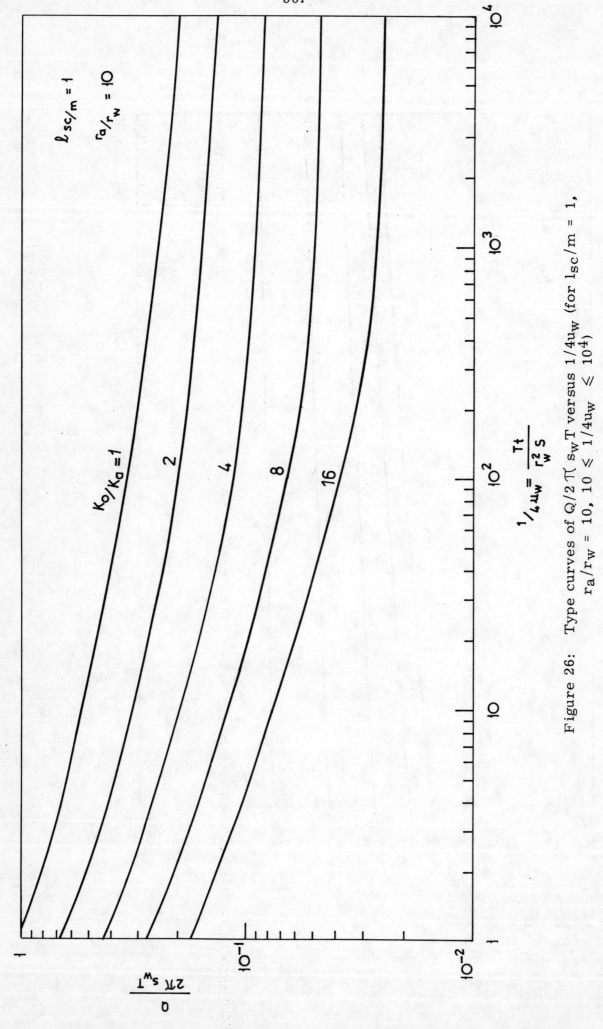

Figure 26: Type curves of $Q/2\pi\, s_w T$ versus $1/4u_w$ (for $l_{sc}/m = 1$, $r_a/r_w = 10$, $10 \leq 1/4u_w \leq 10^4$)

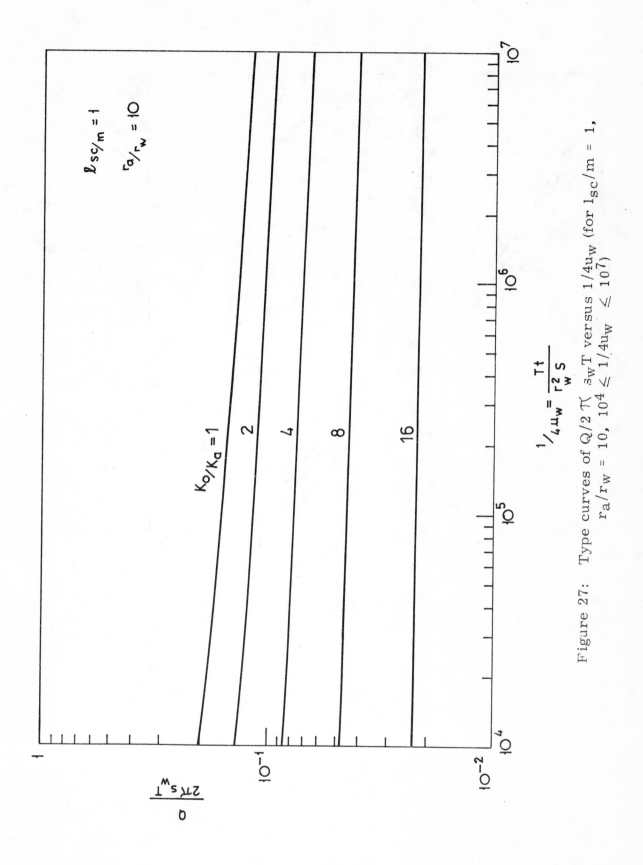

Figure 27: Type curves of $Q/2\pi \ s_w T$ versus $1/4u_w$ (for $l_{sc}/m = 1$, $r_a/r_w = 10$, $10^4 \le 1/4u_w \le 10^7$)

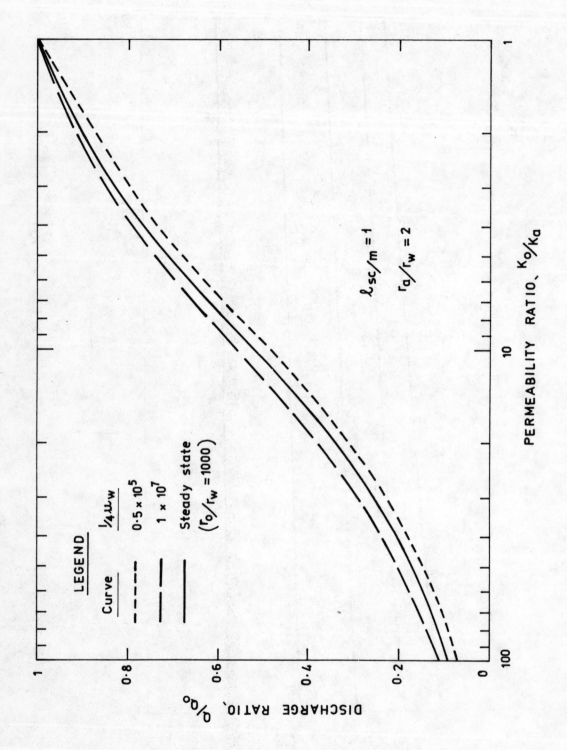

Figure 28: Comparison of transient and steady state type curves of Q/Q_o versus K_o/K_a (for $l_{sc}/m = 1$, $r_a/r_W = 2$)

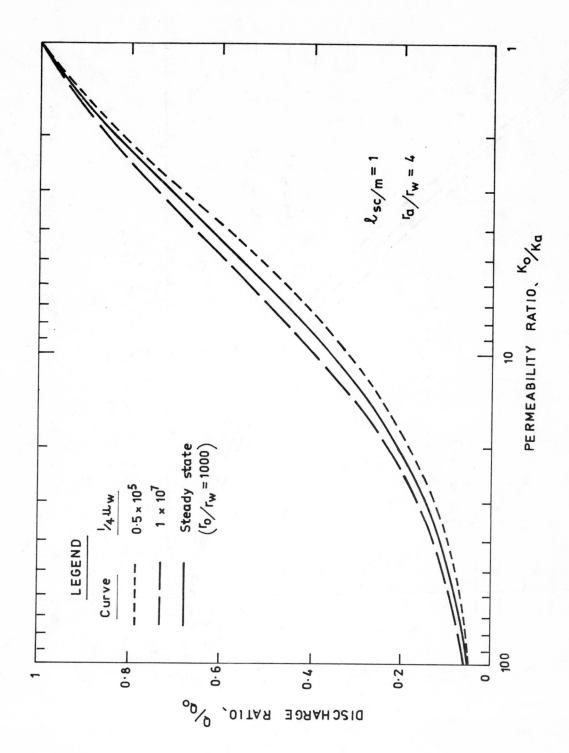

Figure 29:   Comparison of transient and steady state type curves of Q/Q_o versus K_o/K_a (for $l_{sc}/m = 1$, $r_a/r_w = 4$)

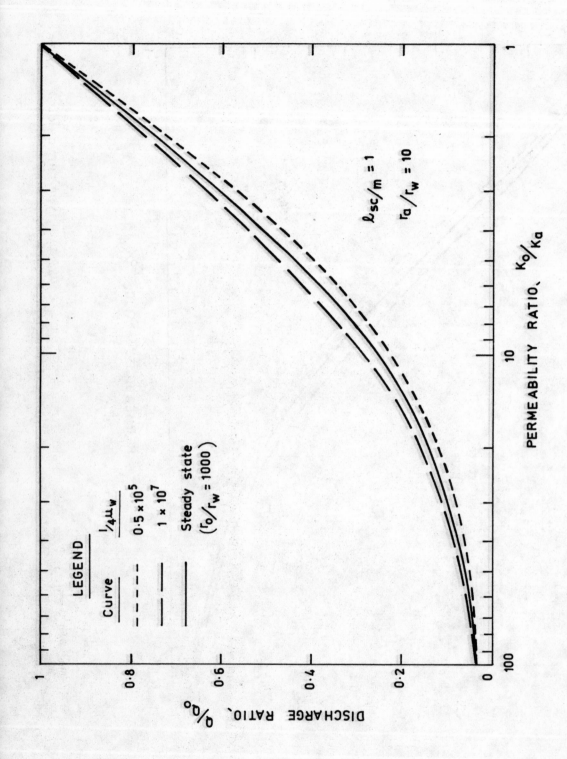

Figure 30: Comparison of transient and steady flow type curves of Q/Q_o versus K_o/K_a (for $l_{sc}/m = 1$, $r_a/r_w = 10$)

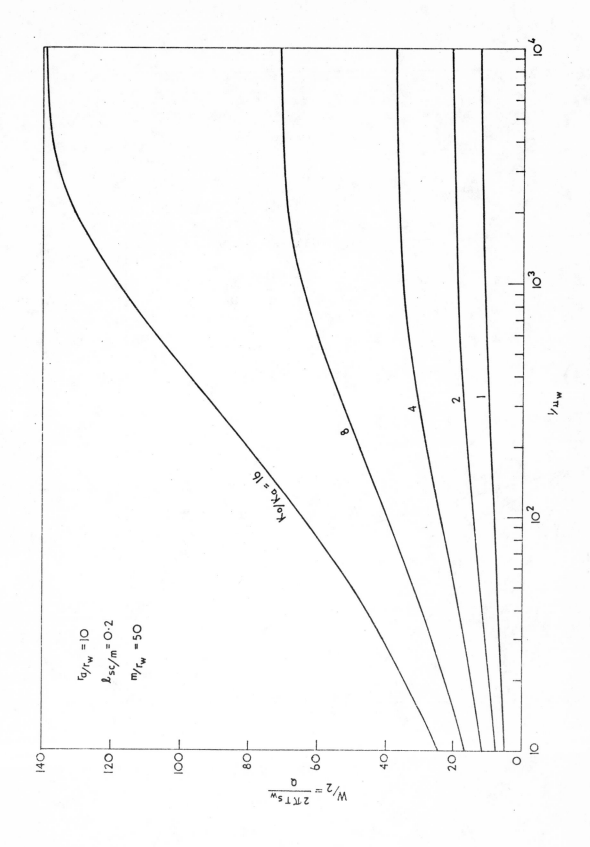

Figure 31: Type curves of $2\pi\, s_w\, T/Q$ versus $1/u_w$ (for $l_{sc}/m = 0.2$, $r_a/r_w = 10$)

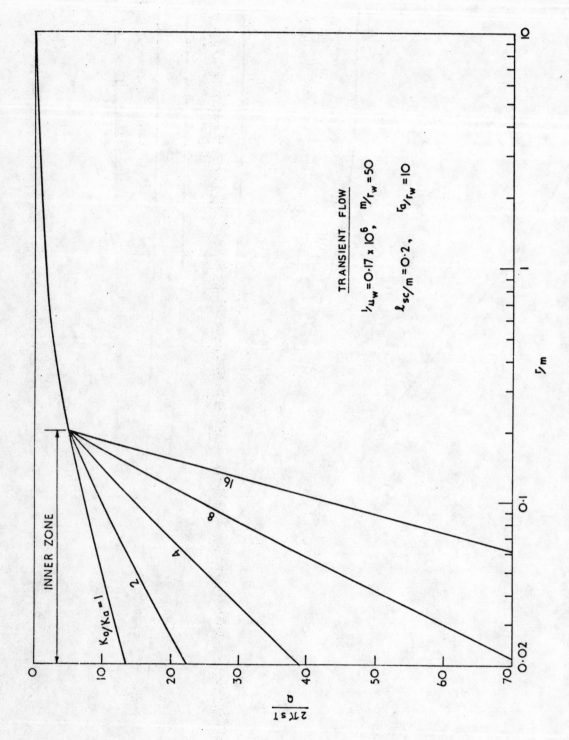

Figure 32: Type curves of $2\pi sT/Q$ versus r/m (transient flow, for $l_{sc}/m = 0.2$, $r_a/r_w = 10$, $1/u_w = 0.17 \times 10^6$

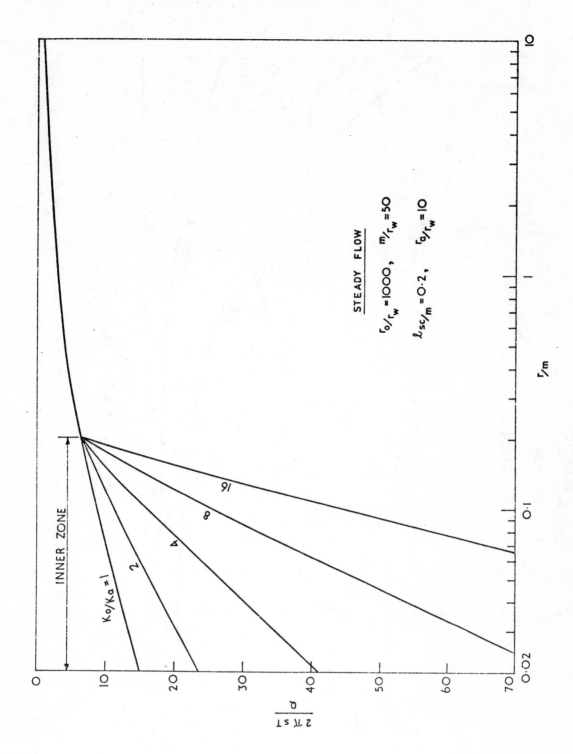

Figure 33:   Type curves of $2\pi sT/Q$ versus r/m (steady flow, for $l_{sc}/m = 0.2$, $r_a/r_w = 10$)

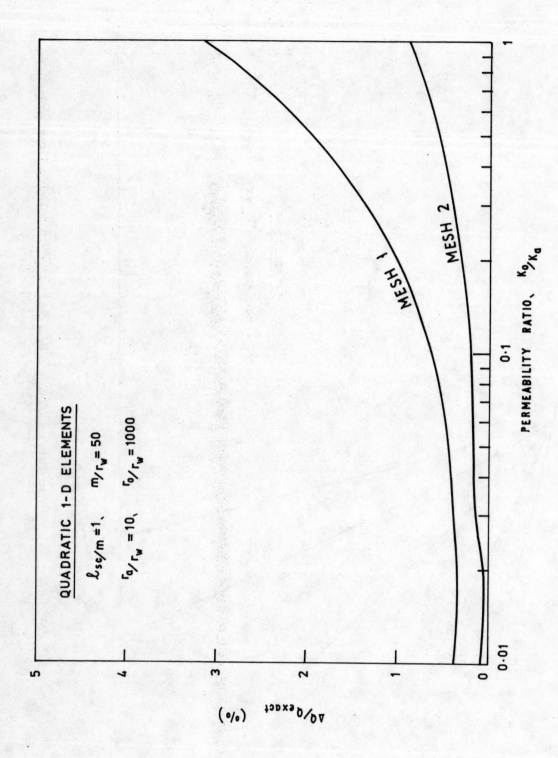

Figure 34: Plot of percentage errors in discharge for the one-dimensional meshes

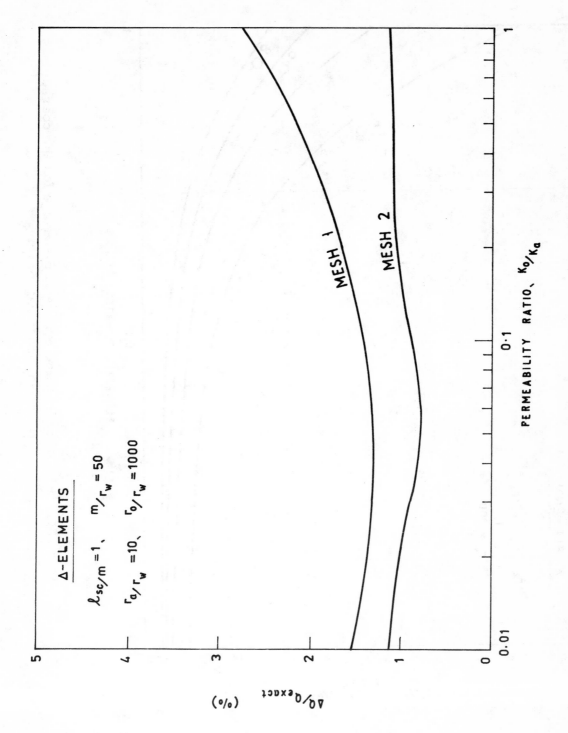

Figure 35: Plot of percentage errors in discharge for the two-dimensional meshes

60.

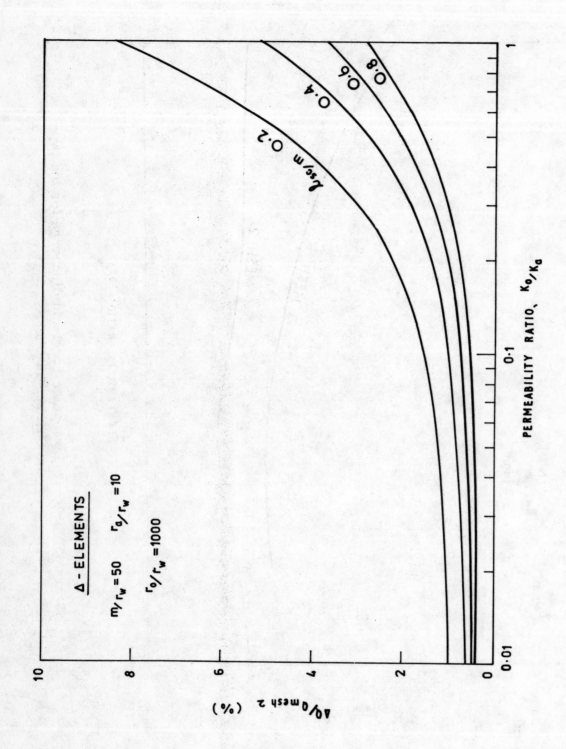

Figure 36: Plot of percentage errors in discharge for the coarse two-dimensional mesh.

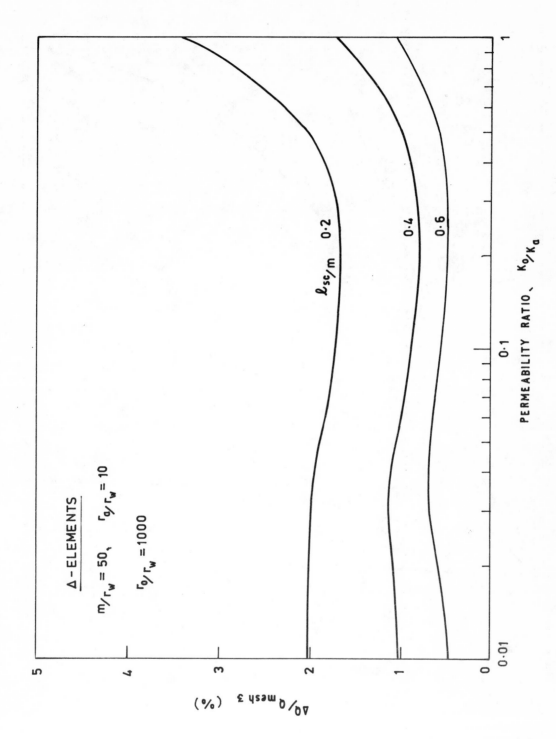

Figure 37: Plot of percentage errors in discharge for the more refined two-dimensional mesh.

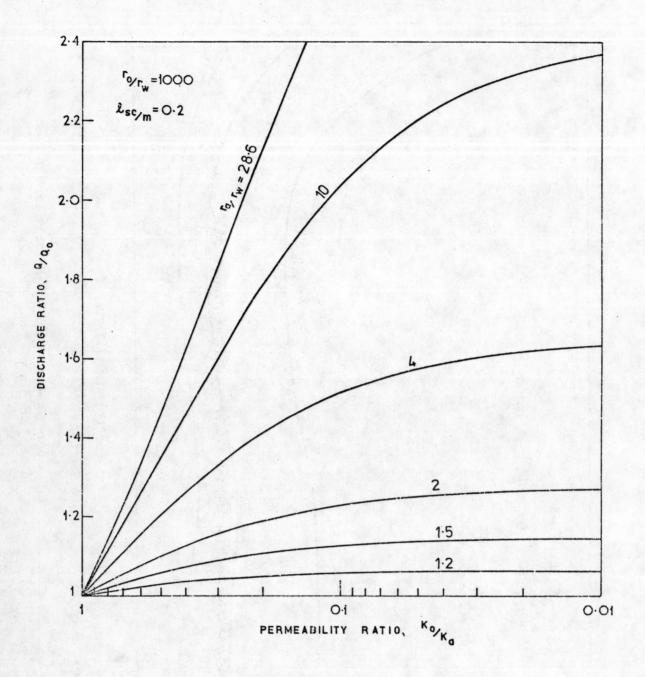

Figure 38: Type curves of Q/Q_o versus K_o/K_a (for $l_{sc}/m = 0.2$)

63.

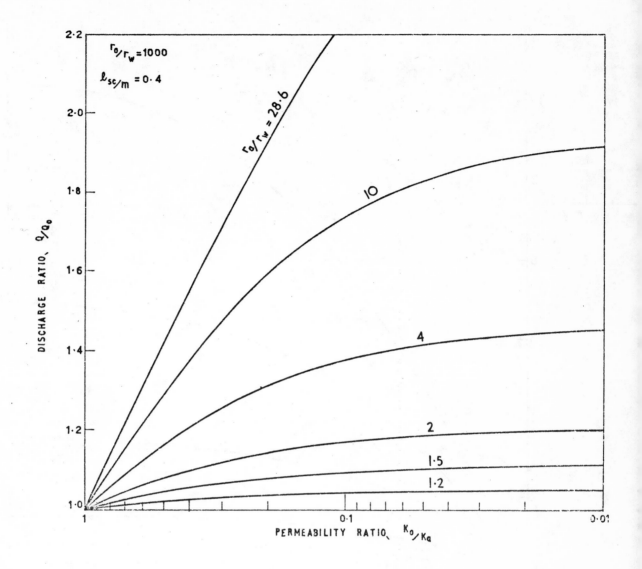

Figure 39: Type curves of Q/Q_O versus K_O/K_a (for $l_{sc}/m = 0.4$)

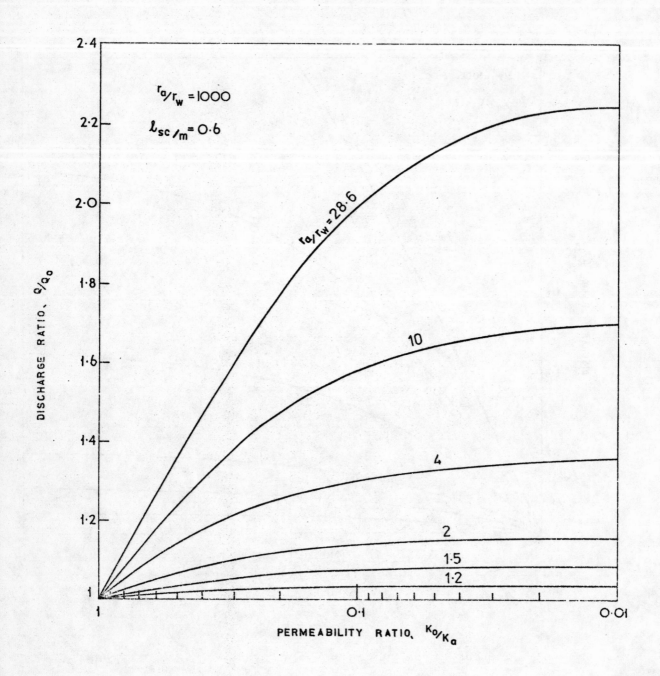

Figure 40: Type curves of Q/Q_0 versus K_0/K_a (for $l_{sc}/m = 0.6$)

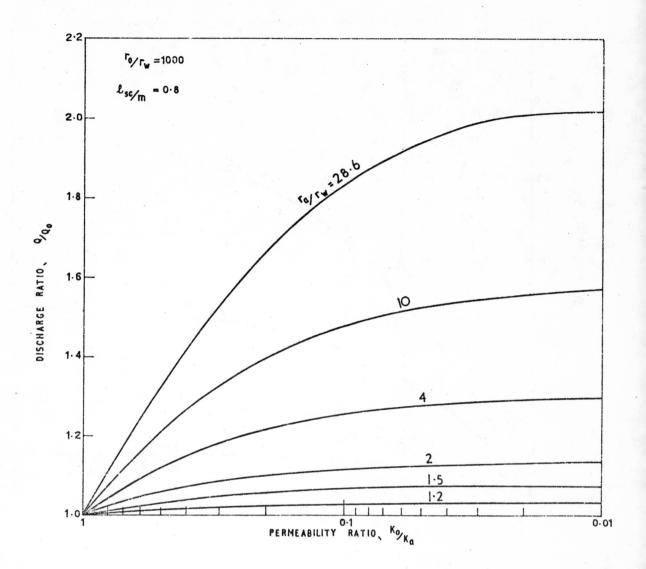

Figure 41:   Type curves of Q/Q_O versus K_O/K_a (for l_{sc}/m = 0.8)

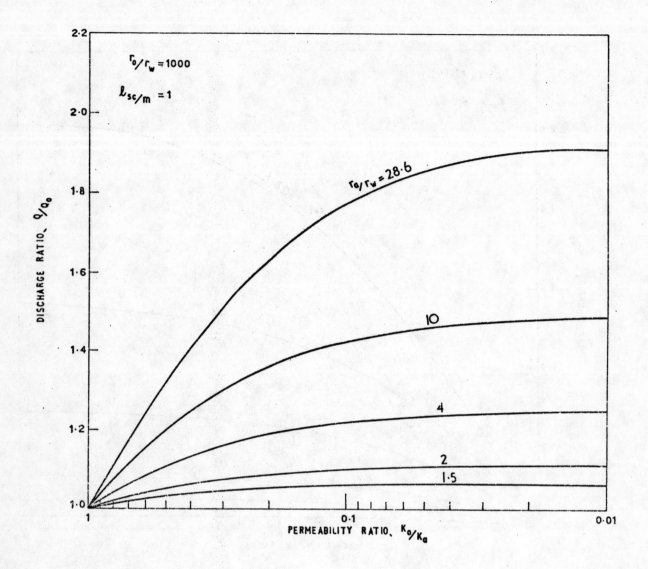

Figure 42:   Type curves of Q/Q_0 versus K_0/K_a (for $l_{sc}/m = 1$)

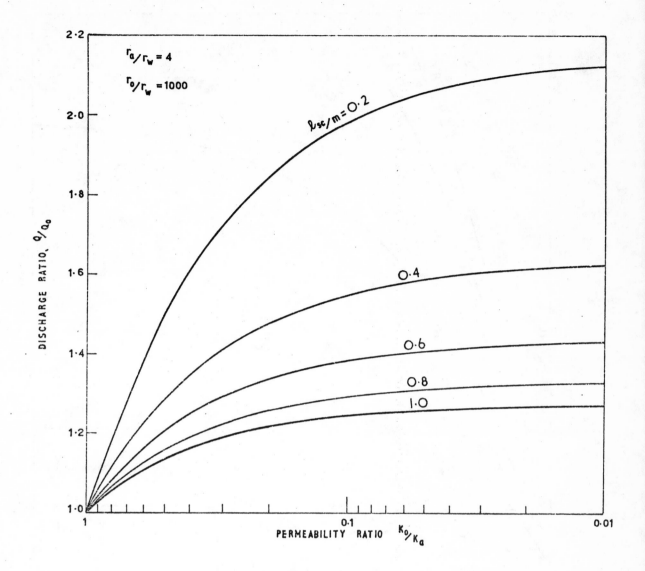

Figure 43:   Comparison of Q/Q_O versus K_O/K_a type curves
for various penetration ratios.

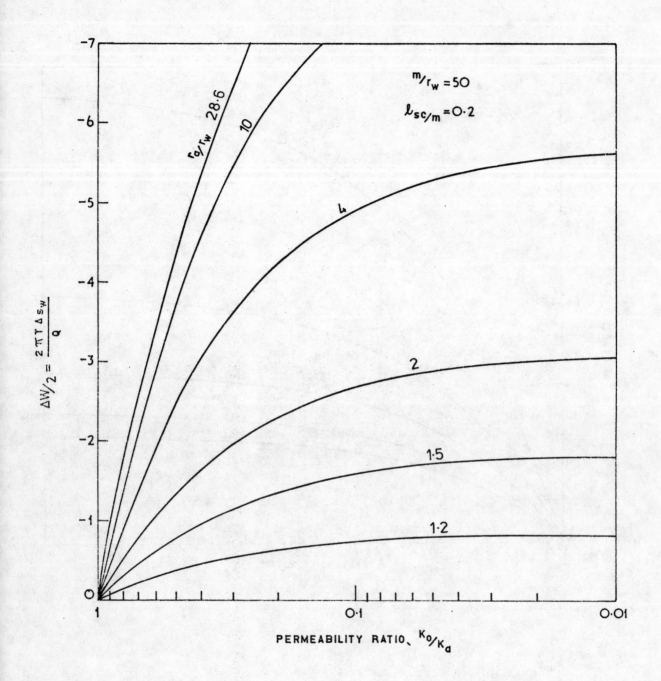

Figure 44:   Type curves of $\Delta w/2$ versus
K_O/K_a (for $l_{sc}/m = 0.2$)

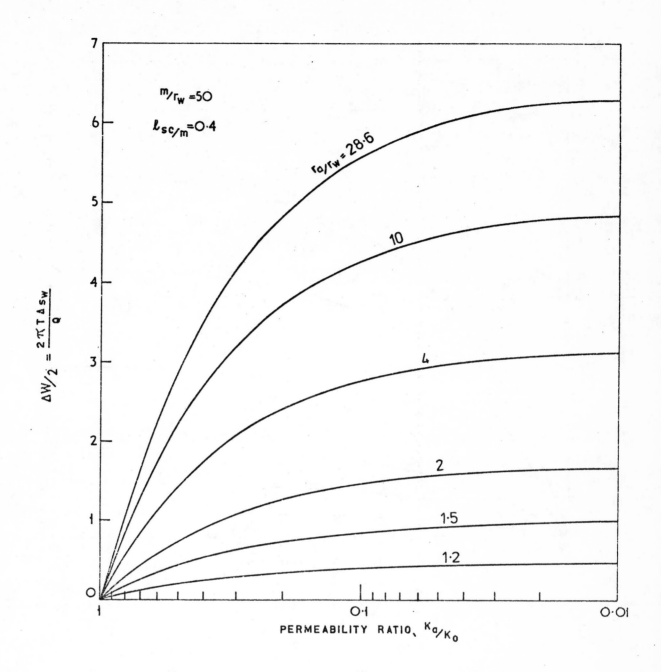

Figure 45: Type curves of $\Delta w/2$ versus
K_O/K_a (for $l_{sc}/m = 0.4$

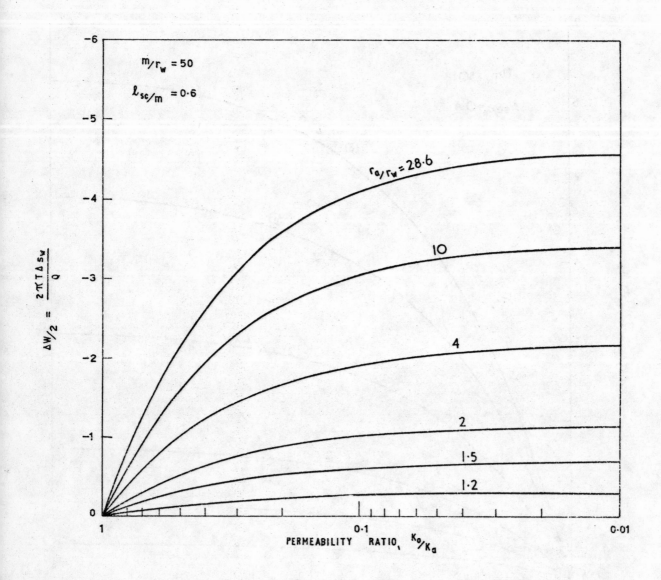

Figure 46: Type curves of $\Delta w/2$ versus K_O/K_a
(for $l_{sc}/m = 0.6$)

71.

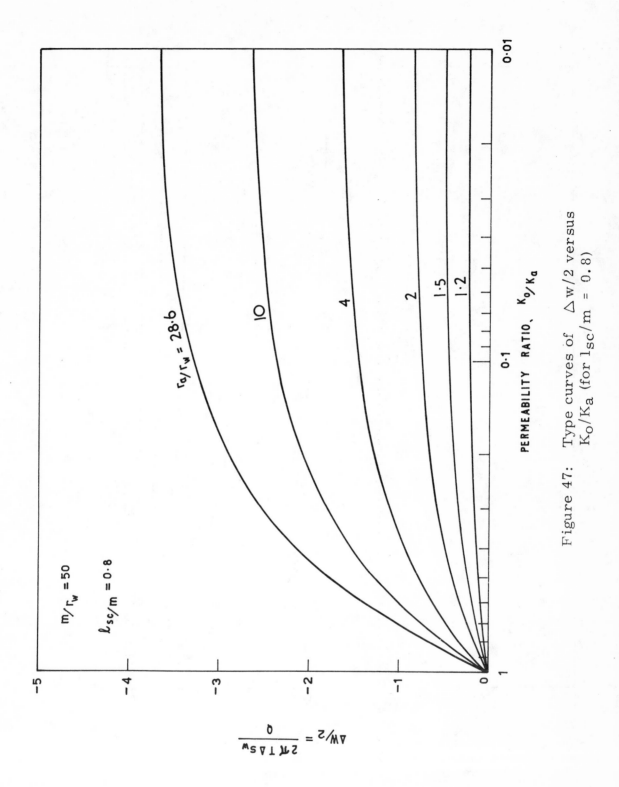

Figure 47:   Type curves of $\Delta w/2$ versus K_O/K_a (for $l_{sc}/m = 0.8$)

72.

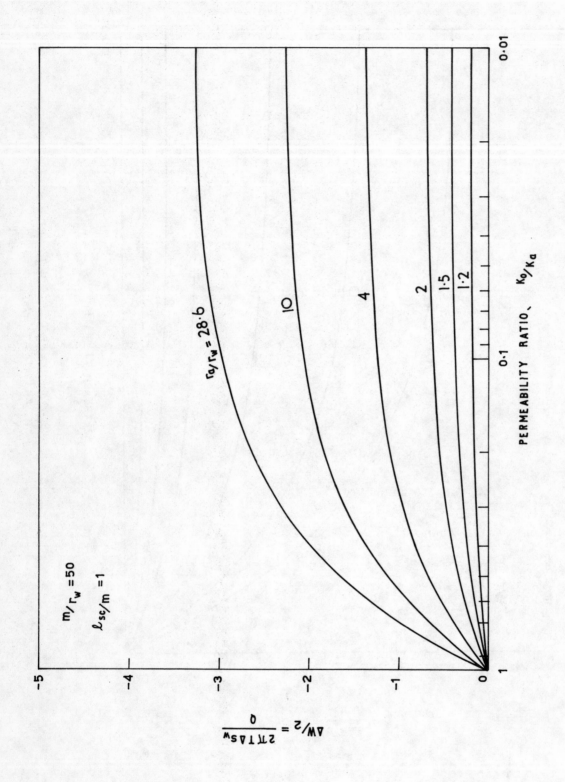

Figure 48: Type curves of $\Delta w/2$ versus
K_o/K_a (for $l_{sc}/m = 1$)

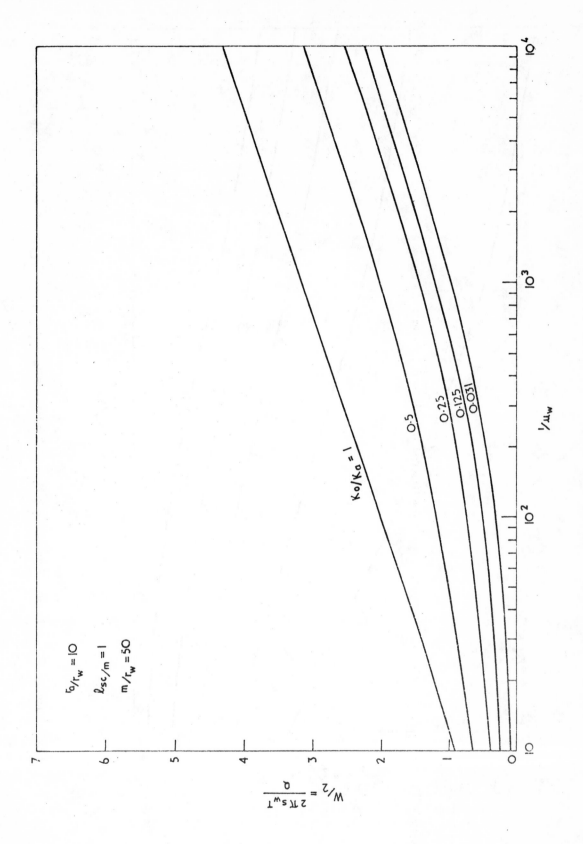

Figure 49: Type curves of $2\pi s_w T/Q$ versus $1/u_w$ (for $l_{sc}/m = 1$, $r_a/r_w = 10$)

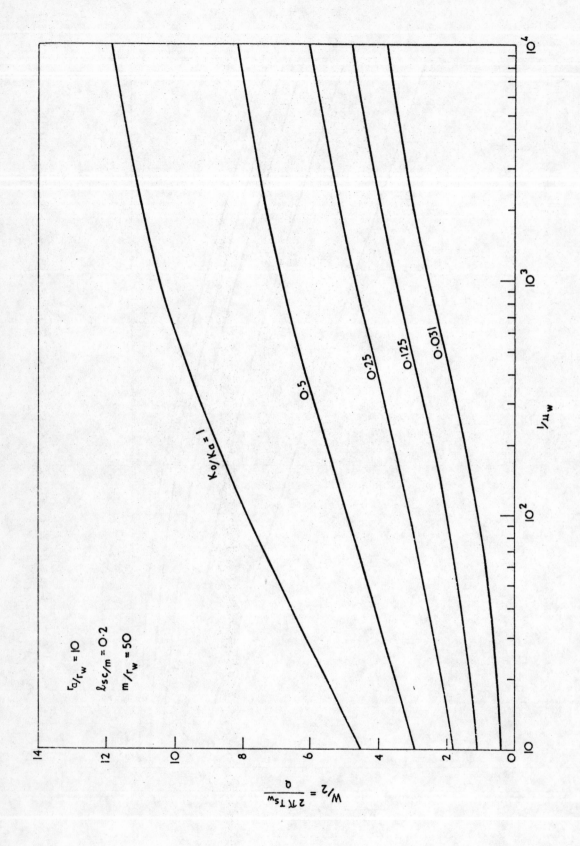

Figure 50: Type curves of $2\pi \, s_w \, T/Q$ versus $1/u_w$ (for $l_{sc}/m = 0.2$, $r_a/r_w = 10$)

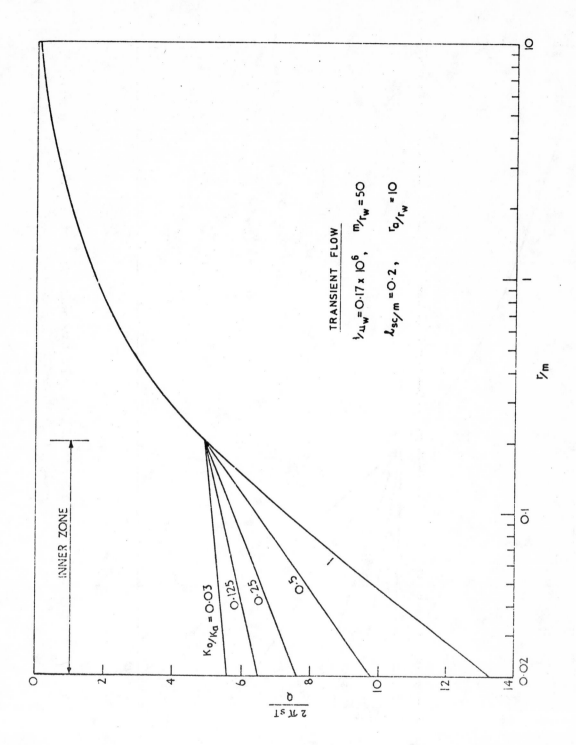

Figure 51: Type curves of $2\pi\,sT/Q$ versus r/m (transient flow, for $l_{sc}/m = 0.2$, $r_a/r_w = 10$, $1/u_w = 0.17 \times 10^6$)

76.

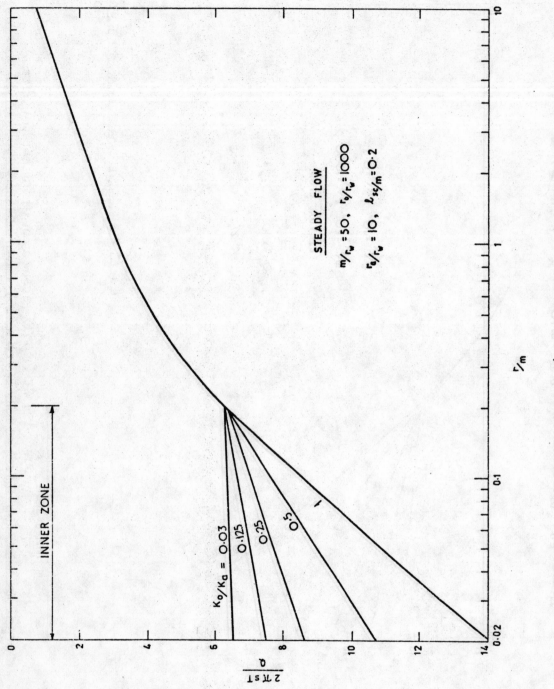

Figure 52: Type curves of $2\pi\ sT/Q$ versus r/m (steady flow, for $l_{sc}/m = 0.2$, $r_a/r_w = 10$)

Appendix   I

Tabulation of Results for Steady Flow with
Permeability Reduction in the Inner Zone.

I-1 Fully Penetrating Wells

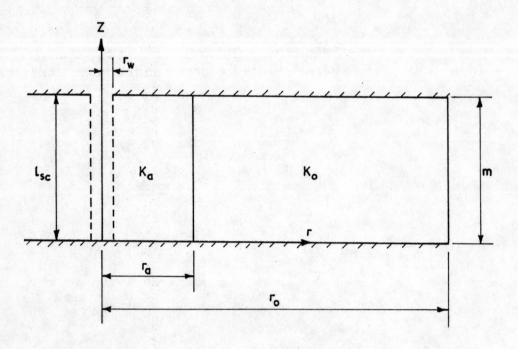

For all finite element results obtained m=50, r_W=1, r_O=1000, $K_O = 0.1$.

Table 1   :   Comparison of Well Discharges computed by
                    finite element method and exact well discharges.

Meshes 1 and 2 are the one-dimensional meshes shown in Fig. 3
Exact well discharges were obtained by applying Equation 2

$$r_a/r_w = 10, \quad l_{sc}/m = 1$$

K_o/K_a	Q-mesh 1	Q-mesh 2	Q-exact
1	469.06	459.06	454.98
2	356.87	345.68	341.23
4	241.39	231.39	227.49
8	146.55	139.29	136.49
16	82.07	77.55	75.83
32	43.65	41.11	40.15
60	24.80	22.56	22.02

| K_o/K_a | $\Delta Q/Q$-exact in (%) | |
	Mesh 1	Mesh 2
1	3.02	0.83
2	4.51	1.24
4	6.04	1.65
8	7.32	2.00
16	8.19	2.23
32	8.69	2.37
60	8.99	2.45

Values of $\Delta Q/Q_{exact}$ are plotted in Fig. 6   against K_o/K_a.

Table 2 : Comparison of well discharges computed by the finite element method and exact well discharges.

Meshes 1 and 2 are the two-dimensional meshes shown in Figs. 4 and 5. Exact well discharges were obtained by using Eq. 2.

$$r_a/r_w = 10, \quad l_{sc}/m = 1$$

K_o/K_a	Q-mesh 1 (FRLEN = 1.89)	Q-mesh 2 (FRLEN = 0.43)	Q-exact
1	467.63	460.12	454.98
2	353.32	346.13	341.23
4	237.31	231.42	227.49
8	143.24	139.16	136.49
16	79.90	77.43	75.83
32	42.40	41.03	40.15
60	23.28	22.51	22.02

K_o/K_a	$\Delta Q/Q_{exact}$ in (%)	
	Mesh 1	Mesh 2
1	2.72	1.00
2	3.49	1.36
4	4.27	1.66
8	4.91	1.90
16	5.32	2.06
32	5.57	2.17
60	5.72	2.22

Values of $\Delta Q/Q_{exact}$ are plotted in Fig. 7 against K_o/K_a

Table   3   :   Mesh data used in preparing type curves.

___

Notation:

FRLEN   =   width of first vertical block

THGP   =   width of inner zone

SCFAC   =   scale factor used for generating the widths of remaining vertical blocks

RGP   =   Outer radius of inner zone

Detailed mesh pattern is depicted in Fig.8.

RGP	THGP	FRLEN	SCFAC
1.1	0.1	0.10	1.50
1.2	0.2	0.08	1.50
1.5	0.5	0.20	1.50
2.0	1.0	0.21	1.50
4.0	3.0	0.37	1.50
10.0	9.0	0.43	1.50
28.6	27.6	0.56	1.50
30.0	29.0	0.59	1.50

Table 4 : Results obtained from two-dimensional mesh 2.

___

The mesh detail is depicted in Fig. 5 . For various values of r_a, corresponding values of FRLEN are listed in Table 3 . Dimensionless type curves in Figs. 14 and 14a were obtained using the results listed in this table.

$$r_a/r_w = 1.1, \; l_{sc}/m = 1$$

K_o/K_a	Q	$2\pi s_w T/Q$	$\Delta W/2$	Q/Q_o
1	459.20	6.84	0	1
2	452.91	6.94	0.10	0.986
4	440.80	7.13	0.29	0.960
8	418.42	7.51	0.67	0.911
16	379.86	8.27	1.43	0.827
32	320.76	9.79	2.95	0.699
60	252.11	12.46	5.62	0.549
100	193.08	16.27	9.43	0.420

$$r_a/r_w = 1.2, \; l_{sc}/m = 1$$

K_o/K_a	Q	$2\pi s_w T/Q$	$\Delta W/2$	Q/Q_o
1	459.20	6.84	0	1
2	447.22	7.02	0.180	0.973
4	425.14	7.39	0.550	0.925
8	386.98	8.12	1.28	0.843
16	328.08	9.58	2.74	0.714
32	251.52	12.49	5.65	0.548
60	178.58	17.59	10.75	0.390
100	126.26	24.88	18.04	0.275

$$r_a/r_w = 1.5, \; l_{sc}/m = 1$$

K_o/K_a	Q	$2\pi s_w T/Q$	$\Delta W/2$	Q/Q_o
1	459.46	6.84	0	1
2	433.83	7.24	0.40	0.944
4	390.27	8.05	1.21	0.849
8	325.01	9.67	2.83	0.707
16	243.56	12.90	6.06	0.530
32	162.25	19.36	12.52	0.353
60	102.41	30.68	23.84	0.223
100	67.07	46.84	40.00	0.146

Table 4 (cont'd.) Results obtained from two-dimensional mesh 2.

$r_a/r_w = 2$, $l_{sc}/m = 1$

$K_o K_a$	Q	$2 \pi s_w T/Q$	$\Delta W/2$	Q/Q_o
1	459.50	6.84	0	1
2	417.46	7.53	0.69	0.909
4	352.85	8.91	2.06	0.768
8	269.43	11.67	4.83	0.586
16	182.95	17.18	10.34	0.398
32	111.42	28.20	21.37	0.242
60	66.15	47.51	40.67	0.144
100	41.86	75.08	68.24	0.091

$r_a/r_w = 4$, $l_{sc}/m = 1$

$K_o K_a$	Q	$2 \pi s_w T/Q$	$\Delta W/2$	Q/Q_o
1	459.91	6.83	0	1
2	382.90	8.20	1.37	0.833
4	286.79	10.95	4.12	0.624
8	190.94	16.45	9.62	0.415
16	114.44	27.45	20.62	0.249
32	63.54	49.44	42.61	0.138
60	35.73	87.92	81.09	.078
100	21.98	142.93	136.10	.048

$r_a/r_w = 10$, $l_{sc}/m = 1$

K_o/K_a	Q	$2 \pi s_w T/Q$	$\Delta W/2$	Q/Q_o
1	460.12	6.83	0	1
2	346.13	9.07	2.25	0.752
4	231.42	13.58	6.75	0.503
8	139.16	22.59	15.76	0.302
16	77.43	40.59	33.76	0.168
32	41.03	76.60	69.77	0.089
60	22.51	139.63	132.80	0.049
100	13.68	229.75	222.92	0.030

$r_a/r_w = 30$, $l_{sc}/m = 1$

K_o/K_a	Q	$2 \pi s_w T/Q$	$\Delta W/2$	Q/Q_o
1	460.59	6.82	0	1
2	310.23	10.13	3.31	0.674
4	187.68	16.74	9.92	0.407
8	104.85	29.96	23.14	0.228
16	55.69	56.41	49.59	0.121
32	28.74	109.31	102.49	0.062
60	15.56	201.90	195.08	0.034
100	9.40	334.21	327.39	0.020

I-2 Partially Penetrating Wells

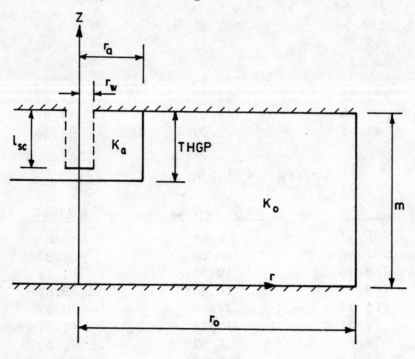

For all finite element results obtained

$$m = 50, \quad r_w = 1, \quad r_o = 1000, \quad THGP = l_{sc} + 2.5, \quad K_O = 0.1$$

Table 5 : Comparison of well discharges obtained using two-dimensional meshes 2 and 3.

Details of mesh 2a are depicted in Fig.8. Mesh 3 is a finer mesh obtained by halving the vertical size of all elements in each regular vertical block shown in Fig. 8

$r_a/r_w = 1.5$, $l_{sc}/m = 0.2$

K_o/K_a	Q-mesh 2a	Q-mesh 3	$\Delta Q/Q$ mesh 3 (%)
1	220.59	210.60	4.74
2	195.26	185.75	5.12
4	159.41	151.28	5.37
8	116.88	110.75	5.53
16	76.30	72.23	5.63
32	45.06	42.63	5.70
60	26.25	24.83	5.71
100	16.44	15.55	5.72

$r_a/r_w = 1.5$, $l_{sc}/m = 0.4$

K_o/K_a	Q-mesh 2a	Q-mesh 3	$\Delta Q/Q$ mesh 3 (%)
1	313.44	306.13	2.39
2	285.44	278.35	2.55
4	242.01	236.60	2.67
8	187.56	182.54	2.75
16	129.03	125.49	2.82
32	79.50	77.27	2.89
60	47.56	46.21	2.92
100	30.22	29.35	2.96

Values of $\Delta Q/Q_{mesh 3}$ are plotted in Fig.9 against K_o/K_a.

$r_a/r_w = 1.5$, $l_{sc}/m = 0.6$

K_o/K_a	Q-mesh 2a	Q-mesh 3	$\Delta Q/Q$ mesh 3 (%)
1	383.32	377.68	1.49
2	354.51	348.93	1.60
4	308.84	303.74	1.68
8	246.02	241.78	1.75
16	175.10	171.96	1.83
32	111.13	109.07	1.89
60	67.81	66.52	1.94
100	43.55	42.72	1.94

Table 5   (cont'd.)   Comparison of well discharges obtained using
two-dimensional meshes 2a and 3.

$r_a/r_w = 1.5$, $l_{sc}/m = 0.8$

K_O/K_a	Q-mesh 2a	Q-mesh 3	$\Delta Q/Q$-mesh 3 (%)
1	435.13	431.21	0.91
2	406.99	402.97	1.00
4	360.80	356.95	1.08
8	294.38	290.98	1.17
16	215.33	212.65	1.26
32	140.15	138.28	1.35
60	87.01	85.80	1.41
100	56.44	55.63	1.45

Values of $\Delta Q/Q$ mesh 3 are plotted in Fig. 9   against K_O/K_a.

Table 6 :   Results obtained for l_{sc}/m = 0.2, 0.4, 0.6 and 0.8 using meshes 2 and 2a.

Details of meshes 2 and 2a are depicted in Figs. 8 and 9   respectively. For r_a/r_w = 4, 10 and 28.6, mesh 2a was used.   For various values of r_a, corresponding values of FRLEN are listed in Table 3   .   The results listed in this table are plotted in Figs. 10 to 14.

r_a/r_w = 1.1, l_{sc}/m = 0.2

K_o/K_a	Q	$2\pi\, s_w\, T/Q$	$\Delta W/2$	Q/Q_o
1	227.05	13.84	0	1
2	219.98	14.28	0.44	0.969
4	207.32	15.15	1.31	0.913
8	186.13	16.88	3.04	0.820
16	154.79	20.30	6.46	0.682
32	115.98	27.09	13.25	0.511
60	80.68	38.94	25.10	0.355
100	56.25	55.85	42.01	0.248

r_a/r_w = 1.2, l_{sc}/m = 0.2

K_o/K_a	Q	$2\pi\, s_w\, T/Q$	$\Delta W/2$	Q/Q_o
1	229.94	13.66	0	1
2	216.47	14.51	0.85	0.941
4	194.21	16.18	2.52	0.845
8	161.48	19.46	5.80	0.702
16	121.03	25.96	12.30	0.526
32	80.74	38.91	25.25	0.351
60	51.04	61.55	47.89	0.222
100	33.47	93.86	80.20	0.146

r_a/r_w = 1.50, l_{sc}/m = 0.2

K_o/K_a	Q	$2\pi\, s_w\, T/Q$	$\Delta W/2$	Q/Q_o
1	220.59	14.24	0	1
2	195.26	16.09	1.85	0.885
4	159.41	19.71	5.47	0.723
8	116.88	26.88	12.64	0.530
16	76.30	41.17	26.93	0.346
32	45.06	69.72	55.48	0.204
60	26.25	119.68	105.44	0.119
100	16.44	191.09	176.85	0.075

Table 6 (cont'd.) Results obtained for l_{sc}/m = 0.2, 0.4, 0.6 and 0.8 using meshes 2 and 2a.

r_a/r_w = 2, l_{sc}/m = 0.2

K_o/K_a	Q	$2\pi s_w T/Q$	$\Delta W/2$	Q/Q_o
1	217.27	14.46	0	1
2	179.01	17.55	3.09	0.824
4	133.06	23.61	9.15	0.612
8	88.13	35.65	21.19	0.406
16	52.65	59.67	45.21	0.242
32	29.17	107.70	93.24	0.134
60	16.39	191.68	177.22	0.075
100	10.08	311.67	297.21	0.046

r_a/r_w = 4, l_{sc}/m = 0.2

K_o/K_a	Q	$2\pi s_w T/Q$	$\Delta W/2$	Q/Q_o
1	210.25	14.94	0	1
2	149.69	20.99	6.05	0.712
4	95.30	32.97	18.03	0.453
8	55.28	56.83	41.89	0.263
16	30.06	104.51	89.57	0.143
32	15.72	199.85	184.91	0.075
60	8.57	366.58	351.64	0.041
100	5.19	605.32	590.38	0.025

r_a/r_w = 10, l_{sc}/m = 0.2

K_o/K_a	Q	$2\pi s_w T/Q$	$\Delta W/2$	Q/Q_o
1	210.30	14.94	0	1
2	133.39	23.55	8.61	0.634
4	77.37	40.60	25.66	0.368
8	42.13	74.57	59.63	0.200
16	22.07	142.35	127.41	0.105
32	11.30	278.01	263.08	0.054
60	6.10	515.02	500.08	0.029
100	3.68	853.70	838.76	0.017

r_a/r_w = 28.6, l_{sc}/m = 0.2

K_o/K_a	Q	$2\pi s_w T/Q$	$\Delta W/2$	Q/Q_o
1	210.57	14.91	0	1
2	127.36	24.66	9.75	0.605
4	72.31	43.45	28.54	0.343
8	39.09	80.37	65.46	0.186
16	20.43	153.77	138.86	0.097
32	10.46	300.34	285.43	0.050
60	5.64	557.02	542.11	0.027
100	3.40	924.00	909.09	0.016

$r_a/r_w = 1.1$, $l_{sc}/m = 0.4$

K_o/K_a	Q	$2\pi\, s_w\, T/Q$	$\Delta W/2$	Q/Q_o
1	318.47	9.86	0	1
2	311.00	10.10	0.24	0.977
4	297.28	10.56	0.71	0.933
8	273.45	11.49	1.63	0.859
16	236.04	13.31	3.45	0.741
32	185.69	16.92	7.06	0.583
60	135.37	23.21	13.35	0.425
100	97.65	32.17	22.31	0.307

$r_a/r_w = 1.2$, $l_{sc}/m = 0.4$

K_o/K_a	Q	$2\pi\, s_w\, T/Q$	$\Delta W/2$	Q/Q_o
1	320.89	9.79	0	1
2	306.66	10.24	0.45	0.956
4	282.18	11.13	1.34	0.879
8	243.88	12.88	3.09	0.760
16	196.27	16.01	6.22	0.612
32	135.33	23.21	13.42	0.421
60	89.20	35.22	25.43	0.278
100	60.00	52.36	42.57	0.187

$r_a/r_w = 1.50$, $l_{sc}/m = 0.4$

K_o/K_a	Q	$2\pi\, s_w\, T/Q$	$\Delta W/2$	Q/Q_o
1	313.44	10.02	0	1
2	285.44	11.01	0.99	0.911
4	242.91	12.93	2.91	0.775
8	187.56	16.75	6.73	0.598
16	129.03	24.35	14.33	0.412
32	79.50	39.52	29.50	0.254
60	47.56	66.06	56.04	0.152
100	30.22	103.96	93.94	0.096

$r_a/r_w = 2$, $l_{sc}/m = 0.4$

K_o/K_a	Q	$2\pi\, s_w\, T/Q$	$\Delta W/2$	Q/Q_o
1	311.19	10.10	0	1
2	267.54	11.74	1.64	0.860
4	209.75	14.98	4.88	0.674
8	146.78	21.40	11.30	0.471
16	91.80	34.22	24.12	0.295
32	52.50	59.84	49.74	0.169
60	30.02	104.65	94.55	0.096
100	18.62	168.72	158.62	0.060

$r_a/r_w = 4$, $l_{sc}/m = 0.4$

K_o/K_a	Q	$2\pi s_w T/Q$	$\Delta W/2$	Q/Q_o
1	305.73	10.28	0	1
2	232.45	13.52	3.24	0.760
4	157.63	19.93	9.65	0.516
8	96.02	32.72	22.44	0.314
16	53.92	58.26	47.98	0.176
32	28.73	109.35	99.07	0.094
60	15.81	198.71	188.43	0.052
100	9.63	326.23	315.95	0.031

$r_a/r_w = 10$, $l_{sc}/m = 0.4$

K_o/K_a	Q	$2\pi s_w T/Q$	$\Delta W/2$	Q/Q_o
1	305.89	10.27	0	1
2	207.01	15.18	4.91	0.677
4	126.05	24.92	14.65	0.412
8	70.81	44.37	34.10	0.231
16	37.75	83.22	72.95	0.123
32	19.52	160.94	150.67	0.064
60	10.58	296.94	286.67	0.035
100	6.40	490.88	480.61	0.021

$r_a/r_w = 28.6$, $l_{sc}/m = 0.4$

K_o/K_a	Q	$2\pi s_w T/Q$	$\Delta W/2$	Q/Q_o
1	306.29	10.26	0	1
2	192.56	16.31	6.05	0.629
4	111.77	28.10	17.84	0.365
8	61.14	51.38	41.12	0.200
16	32.16	97.69	87.43	0.105
32	16.52	190.17	179.91	0.054
60	8.93	351.80	341.54	0.029
100	5.39	582.86	572.59	0.018

$r_a/r_w = 1.1$, $l_{sc}/m = 0.6$

K_o/K_a	Q	$2\pi T s_w/Q$	$\Delta W/2$	Q/Q_o
1	386.93	8.12	0	1
2	379.46	8.28	0.16	0.981
4	365.52	8.59	0.47	0.945
8	340.74	9.22	1.10	0.881
16	300.43	10.46	2.34	0.776
32	243.31	12.91	4.79	0.629
60	182.77	17.19	9.07	0.472
100	134.90	23.29	15.17	0.349

$r_a/r_w = 1.2$, $l_{sc}/m = 0.6$

K_O/K_a	Q	$2\pi T s_w/Q$	$\Delta W/2$	Q/Q_O
1	388.58	8.08	0	1
2	374.37	8.39	0.31	0.963
4	349.31	8.99	0.91	0.900
8	308.59	10.18	2.10	0.794
16	250.69	12.53	4.45	0.645
32	182.56	17.21	9.13	0.470
60	123.81	25.37	17.29	0.319
100	84.84	37.03	28.95	0.218

$r_a/r_w = 1.50$, $l_{sc}/m = 0.6$

K_O/K_a	Q	$2\pi s_w T/Q$	$\Delta W/2$	Q/Q_O
1	383.32	8.20	0	1
2	354.51	8.86	0.66	0.924
4	308.84	10.17	1.97	0.806
8	246.02	12.77	4.57	0.642
16	175.10	17.94	9.74	0.457
32	111.13	28.27	20.07	0.290
60	67.81	46.33	38.13	0.177
100	43.55	72.14	63.94	0.114

$r_a/r_w = 2$, $l_{sc}/m = 0.6$

K_O/K_a	Q	$2\pi s_w T/Q$	$\Delta W/2$	Q/Q_O
1	381.70	8.23	0	1
2	336.03	9.35	1.12	0.880
4	271.93	11.55	3.32	0.712
8	197.17	15.93	7.70	0.517
16	127.32	24.67	16.44	0.334
32	74.54	42.15	33.92	0.195
60	43.21	72.71	64.48	0.113
100	27.00	116.36	108.13	0.071

$r_a/r_w = 4$, $l_{sc}/m = 0.6$

K_O/K_a	Q	$2\pi s_w T/Q$	$\Delta W/2$	Q/Q_O
1	377.56	8.32	0	1
2	298.41	10.53	2.21	0.790
4	210.76	14.91	6.59	0.558
8	132.91	23.64	15.32	0.352
16	76.48	41.08	32.76	0.203
32	41.36	75.96	67.64	0.110
60	22.93	137.01	128.69	0.061
100	14.01	224.24	215.92	0.037

$r_a/r_w = 10$, $l_{sc}/m = 0.6$

K_o/K_a	Q	$2\pi s_w T/Q$	$\Delta W/2$	Q/Q_o
1	377.77	8.32	0	1
2	267.51	11.74	3.42	0.708
4	169.22	18.57	10.25	0.448
8	97.62	32.18	23.86	0.258
16	52.89	59.40	51.08	0.140
32	27.60	113.83	105.51	0.073
60	15.03	209.02	200.70	0.040
100	9.10	345.23	336.91	0.024

$r_a/r_w = 28.6$, $l_{sc}/m = 0.6$

K_o/K_a	Q	$2\pi s_w T/Q$	$\Delta W/2$	Q/Q_o
1	378.16	8.31	0	1
2	246.27	12.76	4.45	0.651
4	146.40	21.46	13.15	0.387
8	81.25	38.67	30.36	0.215
16	43.08	72.92	64.61	0.114
32	22.23	141.32	133.01	0.059
60	12.04	260.93	252.62	0.032
100	7.27	432.13	423.82	0.019

$r_a/r_w = 1.1$, $l_{sc}/m = 0.8$

K_o/K_a	Q	$2\pi T s_w/Q$	$\Delta W/2$	Q/Q_o
1	437.38	7.18	0	1
2	430.24	7.30	0.12	0.984
4	416.76	7.54	0.36	0.953
8	392.32	8.01	0.83	0.897
16	351.39	8.94	1.76	0.803
32	290.99	10.80	3.62	0.665
60	223.86	14.03	6.85	0.512
100	168.42	18.65	11.47	0.385

$r_a/r_w = 1.2$, $l_{sc}/m = 0.8$

K_o/K_a	Q	$2\pi T s_w/Q$	$\Delta W/2$	Q/Q_o
1	438.31	7.17	0	1
2	424.75	7.40	0.23	0.969
4	400.33	7.85	0.68	0.922
8	359.39	8.74	1.57	0.820
16	298.69	10.52	3.35	0.681
32	223.48	14.06	6.89	0.510
60	155.20	20.24	13.07	0.354
100	108.60	28.93	21.76	0.248

$r_a/r_w = 1.50$, $l_{sc}/m = 0.8$

K_o/K_a	Q	$2\pi\, s_w\, T/Q$	$\Delta W/2$	Q/Q_o
1	435.13	7.22	0	1
2	406.99	7.22	0.50	0.935
4	360.80	8.71	1.49	0.829
8	294.38	10.67	3.45	0.677
16	215.33	14.59	7.37	0.495
32	140.15	22.42	15.20	0.322
60	87.01	36.11	28.89	0.200
100	56.44	55.66	48.44	0.130

$r_a/r_w = 2.0$, $l_{sc}/m = 0.8$

K_o/K_a	Q	$2\pi\, s_w\, T/Q$	$\Delta W/2$	Q/Q_o
1	434.14	7.24	0	1
2	388.94	8.08	0.84	0.896
4	322.41	9.74	2.50	0.743
8	240.48	13.06	5.82	0.554
16	159.52	19.69	12.45	0.367
32	95.36	32.94	25.70	0.220
60	55.97	56.13	48.89	0.129
100	35.20	89.25	82.01	0.081

$r_a/r_w = 4$, $l_{sc}/m = 0.8$

K_o/K_a	Q	$2\pi\, s_w\, T/Q$	$\Delta W/2$	Q/Q_o
1	431.47	7.28	0	1
2	351.07	8.95	1.67	0.814
4	256.09	12.27	4.99	0.594
8	166.29	18.89	11.61	0.385
16	97.77	32.13	24.85	0.227
32	53.60	58.61	51.33	0.124
60	29.93	104.96	97.68	0.069
100	18.36	171.11	163.83	0.043

$r_a/r_w = 10$, $l_{sc} = 0.8$

K_o/K_a	Q	$2\pi\, T s_w/Q$	$\Delta W/2$	Q/Q_o
1	431.76	7.28	0	1
2	317.04	9.91	2.63	0.734
4	207.30	15.15	7.87	0.480
8	122.57	25.63	18.35	0.284
16	67.46	46.57	39.29	0.156
32	35.52	88.45	81.17	0.082
60	19.43	161.69	154.41	0.045
100	11.79	266.46	259.18	0.027

$$r_a/r_w = 28.6, \ l_{sc}/m = 0.8$$

K_o/K_a	Q	$2\pi \, s_w \, T/Q$	$\Delta W/2$	Q/Q_o
1	432.21	7.27	0	1
2	289.91	10.84	3.57	0.671
4	176.46	17.80	10.53	0.408
8	99.63	31.53	24.26	0.231
16	53.43	58.80	51.53	0.124
32	27.76	113.17	105.90	0.064
60	15.09	208.19	200.92	0.035
100	9.13	344.10	336.83	0.021

Appendix II

Tabulation of Results for Transient Flow with
Permeability Reduction in the Inner Zone.

II-1 Fully Penetrating Wells

   (i)   Transient flow under constant discharge

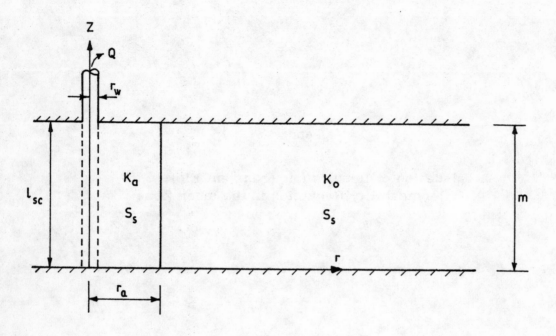

For all finite element results obtained
m = 50, r_w = 1, Q = 100, K_O = 0.1,
S_S = 0.1x10^{-4}

Table   7   :   Results for transient flow towards fully penetrating wells pumped at constant discharge.

The results listed in this table are plotted in Figs. 20   and 21 These results were obtained by using a mesh similar to mesh 2 in Fig.5 but with the external radius r_o = 5000.

$$l_{sc}/m = 1, \quad r_a/r_w = 10$$
$$K_o/K_a = 2$$

Early time results.

$1/u_w$	$(W + \Delta W)/2$	$W/2$	$\Delta W/2$
0.134×10	0.76	0.51	0.25
0.268×10	1.02	0.67	0.35
0.536×10	1.35	0.87	0.48
0.107×10^2	1.74	1.10	0.64
0.214×10^2	2.20	1.36	0.84
0.429×10^2	2.72	1.65	1.07
0.858×10^2	3.29	1.95	1.34
0.172×10^3	3.90	2.27	1.63
0.343×10^3	4.50	2.60	1.90
0.686×10^3	5.03	2.94	2.09
0.137×10^4	5.49	3.28	2.21

Late time results.

$1/u_w$	$(W + \Delta W)/2$	$W/2$	$\Delta W/2$
0.275×10^4	5.88	3.63	2.25
0.549×10^4	6.25	3.97	2.28
0.110×10^5	6.61	4.32	2.29
0.220×10^5	6.96	4.66	2.30
0.439×10^5	7.30	5.00	2.30
0.879×10^5	7.65	5.35	2.30
0.175×10^6	8.00	5.70	2.30
0.352×10^6	8.35	6.05	2.30
0.703×10^6	8.70	6.39	2.31
0.141×10^7	9.04	6.73	2.31
0.281×10^7	9.38	7.08	2.30
0.562×10^7	9.73	7.43	2.30

$\Delta W/2$ for corresponding steady flow case = 2.30

$$l_{sc}/m = 1, \quad r_a/r_w = 10$$

$$K_o/K_a = 4$$

Early time results

$1/u_w$	$(W + \Delta W)/2$	$W/2$	$\Delta W/2$
0.134×10	1.13	0.51	0.62
0.268×10	1.53	0.67	0.86
0.536×10	2.05	0.87	1.18
0.107×10^2	2.70	1.10	1.60
0.214×10^2	3.48	1.36	2.12

0.429×10^2	4.40	1.65	2.75
0.858×10^2	5.44	1.95	3.49
0.172×10^3	6.53	2.27	4.26
0.343×10^3	7.78	2.60	5.18
0.686×10^3	8.90	2.94	5.96
0.137×10^4	9.77	3.28	6.49

Late time results

$1/u_W$	$(W + \Delta W)/2$	$W/2$	$\Delta W/2$
0.275×10^4	10.36	3.63	6.73
0.549×10^4	10.80	3.97	6.83
0.110×10^5	11.18	4.32	6.86
0.220×10^5	11.50	4.66	6.84
0.439×10^5	11.90	5.00	6.90
0.879×10^5	12.25	5.35	6.90
0.175×10^6	12.60	5.70	6.90
0.352×10^6	12.95	6.05	6.90
0.703×10^6	13.30	6.39	6.91
0.141×10^7	13.64	6.73	6.91
0.281×10^7	13.99	7.08	6.91
0.562×10^7	14.33	7.43	6.90

$\Delta W/2$ for corresponding steady flow case = 6.90

$l_{sc}/m = 1$, $r_a/r_W = 10$

$K_o/K_a = 8$

Early time results

$1/u_W$	$(W + \Delta W)/2$	$W/2$	$\Delta W/2$
0.134×10	1.65	0.51	1.14
0.268×10	2.27	0.67	1.60
0.536×10	3.07	0.87	2.20
0.107×10^2	4.10	1.10	3.00
0.214×10^2	5.40	1.36	4.04
0.429×10^2	6.96	1.65	5.31
0.858×10^2	8.80	1.95	6.85
0.172×10^3	10.88	2.27	9.61
0.343×10^3	13.16	2.60	10.56
0.686×10^3	15.53	2.94	12.59
0.137×10^4	17.65	3.28	14.37

Late time results

$1/u_W$	$(W + \Delta W)/2$	$W/2$	$\Delta W/2$
0.275×10^4	19.08	3.63	15.45
0.549×10^4	19.87	3.97	15.90
0.110×10^5	20.34	4.32	16.02
0.220×10^5	20.74	4.66	16.08
0.439×10^5	21.10	5.00	16.10
0.879×10^5	21.45	5.35	16.10

0.175×10^6	21.80	5.70	16.10
0.352×10^6	22.15	6.05	16.10
0.703×10^6	22.49	6.39	16.10
0.141×10^7	22.83	6.73	16.10
0.281×10^7	23.18	7.08	16.10
0.562×10^7	23.53	7.43	16.10

$\Delta W/2$ for corresponding steady flow case = 16.10

$$l_{sc}/m = 1, \quad r_a/r_w = 10$$

$$K_o/K_a = 16$$

Early time results

$1/u_w$	$(W + \Delta W)/2$	$W/2$	$\Delta W/2$
0.134×10	2.39	0.51	1.88
0.268×10	3.32	0.67	2.65
0.536×10	4.54	0.87	3.67
0.107×10^2	6.15	1.10	5.05
0.214×10^2	8.21	1.36	6.85
0.429×10^2	10.79	1.65	9.14
0.858×10^2	13.92	1.95	11.97
0.172×10^3	17.59	2.27	15.32
0.343×10^3	21.75	2.60	19.15
0.686×10^3	26.32	2.94	23.38
0.137×10^4	31.03	3.28	27.75

Late time results

$1/u_w$	$(W + \Delta W)/2$	$W/2$	$\Delta W/2$
0.275×10^4	35.08	3.63	31.45
0.549×10^4	37.52	3.97	33.55
0.110×10^5	38.58	4.32	34.26
0.220×10^5	39.10	4.66	34.44
0.439×10^5	39.49	5.00	34.49
0.879×10^5	39.86	5.35	34.51
0.175×10^6	40.22	5.70	34.52
0.352×10^6	40.57	6.05	34.52
0.703×10^6	40.91	6.39	34.52
0.141×10^7	41.26	6.73	34.53
0.281×10^7	41.61	7.08	34.53
0.562×10^7	41.96	7.43	34.53

$\Delta W/2$ for corresponding steady flow case = 34.52

II-1 Fully Penetrating Wells

(ii) Transient Flow under Constant Drawdown

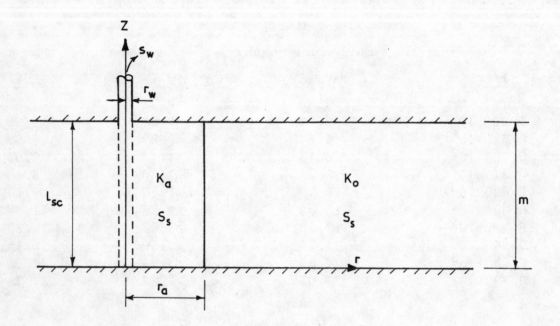

For all finite element results obtained

$m = 50$, $r_W = 1$, $s_W = 100$, $K_O = 0.1$, $S_S = 0.1 \times 10^{-4}$

Table 8 : Values of well function $(1/W = Q/2\pi Ts_w)$
for transient flow under constant drawdown.

Values listed in this table are plotted in Figs. 22 and 23

$l_{sc}/m = 1$, $r_a/r_w = 2$

$1/4u_w$ \ K_o/K_a	1.00	4.00	8.00	16.00
0.10×10	1.047	0.431	0.279	0.186
0.20×10	0.833	0.345	0.212	0.136
0.40×10	0.685	0.300	0.176	0.106
0.80×10	0.577	0.273	0.159	0.0895
0.16×10^2	0.494	0.251	0.150	0.0830
0.32×10^2	0.430	0.232	0.142	0.0800
0.64×10^2	0.379	0.216	0.136	0.0777
0.13×10^3	0.338	0.201	0.130	0.0757
0.26×10^3	0.304	0.189	0.124	0.0737
0.51×10^3	0.277	0.177	0.119	0.0719
0.10×10^4	0.253	0.167	0.115	0.0702
0.20×10^4	0.234	0.158	0.110	0.0685
0.41×10^4	0.216	0.150	0.106	0.0669
0.82×10^4	0.202	0.143	0.102	0.0654
0.16×10^5	0.189	0.136	0.0989	0.0640
0.33×10^5	0.177	0.130	0.0957	0.0626
0.66×10^5	0.167	0.124	0.0926	0.0612
0.13×10^6	0.158	0.119	0.0897	0.0600
0.26×10^6	0.150	0.115	0.0871	0.0588
0.52×10^6	0.143	0.110	0.0845	0.0576
0.10×10^7	0.136	0.106	0.0821	0.0564
0.21×10^7	0.130	0.102	0.0798	0.0554
0.42×10^7	0.124	0.099	0.0777	0.0543
0.84×10^7	0.119	0.096	0.0756	0.0533

Table 9 : Values of well function $(1/W = Q/2\pi Ts_w)$ for transient flow under constant drawdown.

Values listed in this table are plotted in Figs. 24 and 25

$$l_{sc}/m = 1, \quad r_a/r_w = 4$$

K_o/K_a / $1/4\,u_w$	4.00	8.00	16.00	32.00
0.10×10	0.423	0.272	0.172	0.106
0.20×10	0.324	0.207	0.134	0.0849
0.40×10	0.256	0.161	0.103	0.0665
0.80×10	0.208	0.128	0.0804	0.0515
0.16×10^2	0.178	0.104	0.0639	0.0402
0.32×10^2	0.161	0.0904	0.0524	0.0319
0.64×10^2	0.151	0.0836	0.0457	0.0262
0.13×10^3	0.143	0.0803	0.0430	0.0231
0.26×10^3	0.136	0.0778	0.0419	0.0219
0.51×10^3	0.130	0.0757	0.0412	0.0216
0.10×10^4	0.124	0.0738	0.0406	0.0214
0.20×10^4	0.119	0.0719	0.0401	0.0212
0.41×10^4	0.115	0.0702	0.0395	0.0211
0.82×10^4	0.110	0.0685	0.0390	0.0209
0.16×10^5	0.106	0.0669	0.0384	0.0208
0.33×10^5	0.102	0.0654	0.0379	0.0206
0.66×10^5	0.099	0.0640	0.0374	0.0205
0.13×10^6	0.0957	0.0626	0.0370	0.0203
0.26×10^6	0.0926	0.0613	0.0365	0.0202
0.52×10^6	0.0898	0.0600	0.0360	0.0200
0.10×10^7	0.0871	0.0588	0.0356	0.0199
0.21×10^7	0.0845	0.0576	0.0352	0.0198
0.42×10^7	0.0821	0.0565	0.0347	0.0196
0.84×10^7	0.0799	0.0554	0.0343	0.0195

Table 10 : Values of well function $(1/W = Q/2\pi Ts_W)$ for
transient flow under constant drawdown.

Values listed in this table are plotted in Figs.26 and 27

$$l_{sc}/m = 1, \quad r_a/r_W = 10$$

K_o/K_a \ $1/4u_W$	2.00	4.00	8.00	16.00
0.10×10	0.660	0.423	0.272	0.172
0.20×10	0.514	0.324	0.207	0.134
0.40×10	0.415	0.256	0.161	0.103
0.80×10	0.342	0.207	0.128	0.0804
0.16×10^2	0.288	0.171	0.103	0.0638
0.32×10^2	0.247	0.144	0.0856	0.0517
0.64×10^2	0.217	0.124	0.0721	0.0428
0.13×10^3	0.197	0.110	0.0620	0.0360
0.26×10^3	0.182	0.101	0.0554	0.0310
0.51×10^3	0.171	0.0966	0.0520	0.0279
0.12×10^4	0.159	0.0924	0.0501	0.0263
0.24×10^4	0.151	0.0894	0.0491	0.0259
0.48×10^4	0.144	0.0867	0.0483	0.0256
0.96×10^4	0.137	0.0842	0.0475	0.0253
0.19×10^5	0.131	0.0818	0.0467	0.0251
0.38×10^5	0.125	0.0795	0.0459	0.0249
0.77×10^5	0.120	0.0774	0.0452	0.0247
0.15×10^6	0.115	0.0754	0.0445	0.0245
0.31×10^6	0.111	0.0735	0.0438	0.0243
0.61×10^6	0.107	0.0716	0.0432	0.0241
0.12×10^7	0.103	0.0699	0.0426	0.0239
0.25×10^7	0.0994	0.0683	0.0419	0.0237
0.49×10^7	0.0962	0.0667	0.0413	0.0235
0.98×10^7	0.0931	0.0652	0.0407	0.0233

II-2 Partially Penetrating Wells

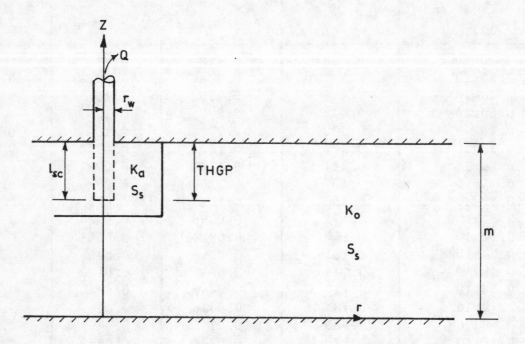

For all finite element results obtained $m = 50$, $r_w = 1$,
THGP $= l_{sc} + 2.5$, $Q = 100$, $K_O = 0.1$, $S_S = 0.1 \times 10^{-4}$.

Table   11   :   Results for transient flow towards partially
penetrating wells pumped at constant discharge.

The results listed in this table are plotted in Fig . 31
These results were obtained by using a mesh similar to mesh 2 in Fig.5
but with the external radius r_o = 5000.

l_{sc}/m = 0.2, r_a/r_w = 10
K_o/K_a = 2

Early time results

$1/u_w$	$(W + \Delta W)/2$	$W/2$	$\Delta W/2$
0.335×10	4.77	3.14	1.63
0.671×10	6.38	4.08	2.30
0.134×10^2	8.19	5.09	3.10
0.268×10^2	10.19	6.16	4.03
0.536×10^2	12.27	7.25	5.02
0.107×10^3	14.43	8.29	6.14
0.214×10^3	16.36	9.24	7.12
0.429×10^3	17.93	10.06	7.87
0.858×10^3	19.00	10.72	8.28
0.172×10^4	19.68	11.24	8.44

Late time results

$1/u_w$	$(W + \Delta W)/2$	$W/2$	$\Delta W/2$
0.536×10^4	20.32	11.84	8.49
0.107×10^5	20.65	12.20	8.46
0.215×10^5	21.01	12.52	8.50
0.429×10^5	21.43	12.83	8.61
0.858×10^5	21.71	13.18	8.53
0.172×10^6	22.12	13.51	8.61
0.343×10^6	22.35	13.81	8.54
0.687×10^6	22.70	14.16	8.54
0.137×10^7	23.11	14.49	8.62
0.275×10^7	23.34	14.80	8.54

$\Delta W/2$ for corresponding steady flow case = 8.61

$l_{sc}/m = 0.2$, $r_a/r_w = 10$

$K_o/K_a = 4$

Early time results

$1/u_w$	$(W + \Delta W)/2$	$W/2$	$\Delta W/2$
0.335×10	7.03	3.14	3.89
0.671×10	9.69	4.08	5.61
0.134×10^2	12.80	5.09	7.71
0.268×10^2	16.39	6.16	10.23
0.536×10^2	20.36	7.25	13.11
0.107×10^3	24.51	8.29	16.22
0.214×10^3	28.76	9.24	19.52
0.429×10^3	32.31	10.06	22.25
0.858×10^3	34.90	10.72	24.18
0.172×10^4	36.28	11.24	25.04

Late time results

$1/u_w$	$(W + \Delta W)/2$	$W/2$	$\Delta W/2$
0.536×10^4	37.21	11.84	25.37
0.107×10^5	37.73	12.20	25.53
0.215×10^5	37.90	12.52	25.38
0.429×10^5	38.20	12.83	25.37
0.858×10^5	38.59	13.18	25.41
0.172×10^6	39.03	13.51	25.52
0.343×10^6	39.21	13.81	25.40
0.687×10^6	39.54	14.16	25.38
0.137×10^7	39.93	14.49	25.44
0.275×10^7	40.38	14.80	25.58

$\Delta W/2$ for corresponding steady flow case = 25.66

$l_{sc}/m = 0.2$, $r_a/r_w = 10$

$K_o/K_a = 8$

Early time results

$1/u_w$	$(W + \Delta W)/2$	$W/2$	$\Delta W/2$
0.335×10	10.03	3.14	6.89
0.671×10	14.30	4.08	10.22
0.134×10^2	19.45	5.09	14.36
0.268×10^2	25.61	6.16	19.45
0.536×10^2	32.76	7.25	25.51
0.107×10^3	40.69	8.29	32.40
0.214×10^3	48.97	9.24	39.73

0.429×10^3	57.09	10.06	47.03
0.858×10^3	63.98	10.72	53.26
0.172×10^4	68.36	11.24	57.12

Late time results

$1/u_W$	$(W + \Delta W)/2$	$W/2$	$\Delta W/2$
0.536×10^4	70.46	11.84	59.01
0.107×10^5	71.00	12.20	58.80
0.215×10^5	71.47	12.52	58.94
0.429×10^5	71.83	12.83	59.00
0.858×10^5	72.10	13.18	58.92
0.172×10^6	72.44	13.51	58.93
0.343×10^6	72.70	13.81	58.89
0.687×10^6	73.00	14.16	58.84
0.137×10^7	73.36	14.49	58.87
0.275×10^7	73.78	14.80	58.98

$\Delta W/2$ for corresponding steady flow case = 59.63

$l_{sc}/m = 0.2, \quad r_a/r_W = 10$

$K_O/K_a = 16$

Early time results

$1/u_W$	$(W + \Delta W)/2$	$W/2$	$\Delta W/2$
0.335×10	13.79	3.14	10.65
0.671×10	20.72	4.08	16.64
0.134×10^2	29.08	5.09	23.99
0.268×10^2	39.40	6.16	33.24
0.536×10^2	51.88	7.25	44.63
0.107×10^3	66.35	8.29	58.06
0.214×10^3	82.37	9.24	73.13
0.429×10^3	99.09	10.06	89.03
0.858×10^3	115.29	10.72	104.57
0.172×10^4	128.66	11.24	117.42

Late time results

$1/u_W$	$(W + \Delta W)/2$	$W/2$	$\Delta W/2$
0.536×10^4	138.08	11.84	126.25
0.107×10^5	138.60	12.20	126.41
0.215×10^5	139.17	12.52	126.65
0.429×10^5	139.83	12.83	127.00
0.858×10^5	139.94	13.18	126.76
0.172×10^6	140.60	13.51	127.09

$\Delta W/2$ for corresponding steady flow case = 127.41

Appendix III

Tabulation of Results for Steady Flow with Permeability
Improvement in the Inner Zone.

III-1 Fully Penetrating Wells

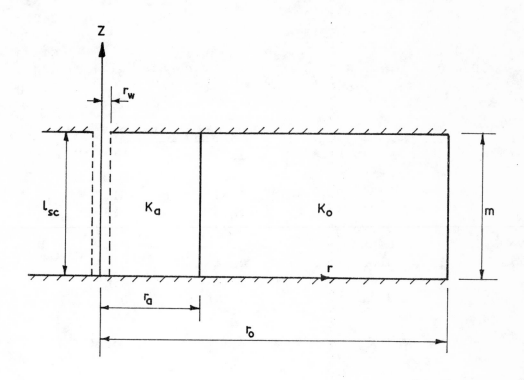

For all finite element results obtained
m = 50, r_W=1, r_O = 1000, K_O = 0.1.

Table 12 : Comparison of well discharges computed by the finite
element method and exact well discharges.

Meshes 1 and 2 are the one-dimensional meshes shown in Fig. 3
Exact well discharges were obtained by applying Eq. (2).

$$r_a/r_w = 10, \; l_{sc}/m = 1$$

K_o/K_a	Q-mesh 1	Q-mesh 2	Q-exact
1	469.06	459.06	454.98
0.5	556.55	549.08	545.97
0.25	613.76	608.88	606.63
0.125	647.10	643.76	642.32
0.062	665.15	663.16	661.94
0.031	674.80	673.10	672.05
0.020	677.88	676.06	675.71
0.010	681.70	679.74	679.07

K_o/K_a	$\Delta Q/Q_{exact}$ (%)	
	Mesh 1	Mesh 2
1	3.18	0.90
0.5	1.94	0.57
0.25	1.18	0.37
0.125	0.74	0.22
0.062	0.48	0.18
0.031	0.41	0.16
0.020	0.32	0.05
0.010	0.39	0.10

Values of $\Delta Q/Q_{exact}$ are plotted in Fig. 34 against K_o/K_a.

Table 13 : Comparison of well discharges computed by the finite
element method and exact well discharges.

Meshes 1 and 2 are the two-dimensional meshes shown in Figs. 4
and 5. Exact well discharges were obtained by applying Eq.(2)

$$r_a/r_w = 10, \ l_{sc}/m = 1$$

K_o/K_a	Q-mesh 1	Q-mesh 2	Q exact
1	467.63	460.16	454.98
0.5	557.85	551.97	545.97
0.25	617.53	613.24	606.63
0.125	652.09	648.89	642.32
0.062	670.77	667.20	661.94
0.031	680.97	678.13	672.05
0.020	685.19	682.62	675.71
0.010	689.70	686.76	679.07

K_o/K_a	$\Delta Q/Q_{exact}$ (%)	
	Mesh 1	Mesh 2
1	2.78	1.14
0.5	2.18	1.10
0.25	1.80	1.09
0.125	1.52	1.02
0.062	1.33	0.79
0.031	1.33	0.90
0.020	1.40	1.02
0.010	1.56	1.13

Table 14 : Results obtained from two-dimensional mesh 2.

The mesh detail is depicted in Fig. 5. For various values of r_a, corresponding values of FRLEN are listed in Table 3 . Dimensionless type curves in Figs. 42 and 43 were obtained using the results listed in this table.

r_a/r_w = 1.1, l_{sc}/m = 1

K_o/K_a	Q	$2\pi Ts_w/Q$	$\Delta W/2$	Q/Q_o
1	459.19	6.84	0	1
0.50	462.51	6.79	-0.05	1.007
0.25	464.19	6.77	-0.07	1.011
0.125	464.77	6.76	-0.08	1.012
0.062	465.00	6.75	-0.09	1.013
0.031	466.16	6.74	-0.10	1.015
0.020	466.89	6.73	-0.11	1.017
0.010	466.89	6.73	-0.11	1.017

r_a/r_w = 1.2, l_{sc}/m = 1

K_o/K_a	Q	$2\pi Ts_w/Q$	$\Delta W/2$	Q/Q_o
1	459.20	6.84	0	1
0.50	465.40	6.75	-0.09	1.014
0.25	468.70	6.70	-0.14	1.021
0.125	470.12	6.68	-0.16	1.023
0.062	471.64	6.66	-0.18	1.027
0.031	471.95	6.66	-0.18	1.028
0.020	472.00	6.65	-0.19	1.028
0.010	472.00	6.65	-0.19	1.028

r_a/r_w = 1.5, l_{sc}/m = 1

K_o/K_a	Q	$2\pi Ts_w/Q$	$\Delta W/2$	Q/Q_o
1	459.46	6.84	0	1
0.50	473.47	-6.64	-0.20	1.030
0.25	480.83	-6.53	-0.31	1.047
0.125	484.59	-6.48	-0.36	1.055
0.062	485.94	-6.46	-0.38	1.058
0.031	487.52	-6.44	-0.40	1.061
0.020	488.52	-6.43	-0.41	1.063
0.010	489.45	-6.42	-0.43	1.063

$r_a/r_w = 2$, $l_{sc}/m = 1$

K_o/K_a	Q	$2\pi s_w T/Q$	$\Delta W/2$	Q/Q_o
1	459.52	6.84	0	1
0.5	483.90	6.49	-0.35	1.053
0.25	497.18	6.32	-0.52	1.082
0.125	504.02	6.23	-0.61	1.097
0.062	506.78	6.20	-0.64	1.103
0.031	508.96	6.17	-0.67	1.107
0.020	509.84	6.16	-0.68	1.110
0.010	513.14	6.12	-0.72	1.116

$r_a/r_w = 4$, $l_{sc}/m = 1$

K_o/K_a	Q	$2\pi s_w T/Q$	$\Delta W/2$	Q/Q_o
1	459.93	6.83	0	1
0.5	511.35	6.14	-0.69	1.112
0.25	541.74	5.80	-1.03	1.178
0.125	558.52	5.62	-1.21	1.214
0.062	566.02	5.55	-1.28	1.231
0.031	570.48	5.51	-1.32	1.240
0.020	573.19	5.48	-1.35	1.246
0.010	576.13	5.45	-1.38	1.253

$r_a/r_w = 10$, $l_{sc}/m = 1$

K_o/K_a	Q	$2\pi s_w T/Q$	$\Delta W/2$	Q/Q_o
1	460.16	6.83	0	1
0.5	551.97	5.69	-1.14	1.200
0.25	613.24	5.12	-1.71	1.333
0.125	648.89	4.84	-1.99	1.410
0.062	667.20	4.71	-2.12	1.450
0.031	678.13	4.63	-2.20	1.474
0.020	682.62	4.60	-2.23	1.483
0.010	686.76	4.57	-2.26	1.492

$r_a/r_w = 28.5$, $l_{sc}/m = 1$

K_o/K_a	Q	$2\pi s_w T/Q$	$\Delta W/2$	Q/Q_o
1	460.59	6.82	0	1
0.5	608.02	5.17	-1.65	1.320
0.25	723.64	4.34	-2.48	1.571
0.125	799.10	3.93	-2.89	1.735
0.062	843.44	3.72	-3.10	1.831
0.031	869.21	3.61	-3.21	1.887
0.020	877.90	3.58	-3.24	1.906
0.010	877.90	3.58	-3.24	1.906

III-2 Partially Penetrating Wells

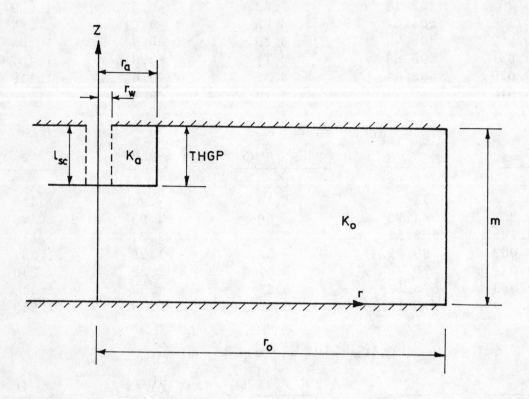

For all finite element results obtained $m = 50$, $r_w = 1$, $r_0 = 1000$,

$THGP = l_{sc}$, $K_O = 0.1$

Table 15 : Comparison of well discharges obtained using two-dimensional meshes 1 and 2.

Details of meshes 1 and 2 are depicted in Figs.4 and 5 The results listed in this table are plotted in Fig.36.

$$r_a/r_w = 10, \quad l_{sc}/m = 0.2$$

K_o/K_a	Q-mesh 1	Q-mesh 2	$\Delta Q/Q$ mesh 2 (%)
1	235.87	217.11	8.64
0.5	304.87	291.32	4.65
0.25	375.46	365.80	2.64
0.125	434.04	426.74	1.71
0.062	474.65	468.43	1.33
0.031	499.59	493.98	1.14
0.020	509.31	503.86	1.08
0.010	518.65	513.62	0.98

$$r_a/r_w = 10, \quad l_{sc}/m = 0.4$$

K_o/K_a	Q-mesh 1	Q-mesh 2	$\Delta Q/Q$ mesh 2(%)
1	327.37	311.11	5.23
0.5	410.81	399.63	2.80
0.25	482.51	474.85	1.61
0.125	534.25	528.65	1.06
0.062	567.04	562.10	0.88
0.031	586.23	581.87	0.75
0.020	593.77	589.54	0.72
0.010	600.83	597.07	0.63

$$r_a/r_w = 10, \quad l_{sc}/m = 0.6$$

K_o/K_a	Q-mesh 1	Q-mesh 2	$\Delta Q/Q$mesh 2 (%)
1	396.11	381.66	3.79
0.5	483.75	474.29	2.04
0.25	552.42	545.98	1.18
0.125	598.20	593.60	0.77
0.062	625.76	621.52	0.68
0.031	641.53	637.92	0.57
0.020	647.96	644.39	0.55
0.010	653.97	650.68	0.50

$$r_a/r_w = 10, \quad l_{sc}/m = 0.8$$

K_o/K_a	Q-mesh 1	Q-mesh 2	$\Delta Q/Q$ mesh 2 (%)
1	446.58	434.17	2.86
0.5	534.08	525.88	1.56
0.25	597.48	592.10	0.91
0.125	637.26	633.50	0.59
0.062	660.16	656.37	0.58
0.031	672.97	669.93	0.45
0.020	678.18	675.32	0.42
0.010	683.43	680.59	0.41

Table 16 : Comparison of well discharges obtained using two-dimensional meshes 2 and 3.

Details of mesh 2 are depicted in Fig. 5. Mesh 3 is a finer mesh obtained by halving the vertical size of all elements in each regular vertical block shown in Fig. 5 The results listed in this table are plotted in Fig. 37.

$r_a/r_w = 10$, $l_{sc}/m = 0.2$

K_o/K_a	Q-mesh 2	Q-mesh 3	$\Delta Q/Q$ mesh 3 (%)
1	217.11	209.00	3.43
0.5	291.32	285.44	2.06
0.25	365.80	359.74	1.68
0.125	426.74	419.52	1.72
0.062	468.43	459.94	1.84
0.031	493.98	484.31	2.00
0.020	503.86	493.91	2.01
0.010	513.62	503.42	2.03

$r_a/r_w = 10$, $l_{sc}/m = 0.4$

K_o/K_a	Q-mesh 2	Q-mesh 3	$\Delta Q/Q$ mesh 3 (%)
1	311.11	305.80	1.74
0.5	399.63	395.63	1.01
0.25	474.85	470.93	0.83
0.125	528.65	523.96	0.87
0.062	562.10	556.56	1.00
0.031	581.87	575.32	1.14
0.020	589.54	583.22	1.08
0.010	597.07	591.07	1.02

$r_a/r_w = 10$, $l_{sc}/m = 0.6$

K_o/K_a	Q-mesh 2	Q-mesh 3	$\Delta Q/Q$ mesh 3 (%)
1	381.66	377.63	1.06
0.5	474.29	471.43	0.61
0.25	545.98	543.31	0.49
0.125	593.60	590.39	0.54
0.062	621.52	617.69	0.62
0.031	637.92	633.22	0.74
0.020	644.39	640.52	0.60
0.010	650.68	647.66	0.47

$r_a/r_w = 10$, $l_{sc}/m = 0.8$

K_o/K_a	Q-mesh 2	Q-mesh 3	$\Delta Q/Q$ mesh 3 (%)
1	434.17	431.47	0.63
0.5	525.88	524.18	0.32
0.25	592.10	590.64	0.25
0.125	633.50	631.76	0.28
0.062	656.37	654.29	0.32
0.031	669.93	666.98	0.44
0.020	675.32	673.81	0.22
0.010	680.59	680.25	0.05

Table 17 : Results obtained for l_{sc}/m = 0.2, 0.4, 0.6 and 0.8 using two-dimensional mesh 2.

Details of mesh 2 are depicted in Fig. 5. For various values of r_a, corresponding values of FRLEN are listed in Table 3 . The results listed in this table are plotted in Figs. 38 to 41.

r_a/r_w = 1.1, l_{sc}/m = 0.2

K_o/K_a	Q	$2\pi Ts_w/Q$	$\Delta W/2$	Q/Q_o
1	227.05	13.84	0	1
0.5	230.26	13.64	-0.20	1.014
0.25	232.18	13.53	-0.31	1.023
0.125	233.23	13.46	-0.38	1.027
0.062	233.83	13.43	-0.41	1.030
0.031	234.30	13.41	-0.43	1.032
0.020	234.34	13.41	-0.43	1.032
0.010	234.34	13.41	-0.43	1.032

r_a/r_w = 1.2, l_{sc}/m = 0.2

K_o/K_a	Q	$2\pi s_w T/Q$	$\Delta W/2$	Q/Q_o
1	229.94	13.66	0	1
0.50	236.32	13.29	-0.37	1.028
0.25	240.25	13.08	-0.58	1.045
0.125	242.51	12.95	-0.71	1.055
0.062	243.89	12.88	-0.78	1.061
0.031	244.63	12.84	-0.82	1.064
0.020	244.63	12.84	-0.82	1.064
0.010	244.63	12.84	-0.82	1.064

r_a/r_w = 1.5, l_{sc}/m = 0.2

K_o/K_a	Q	$2\pi Ts_w/Q$	$\Delta W/2$	Q/Q_o
1	220.59	14.24	0	1
0.50	233.69	13.44	-0.80	1.059
0.25	242.01	12.98	-1.26	1.097
0.125	246.98	12.72	-1.52	1.120
0.062	249.75	12.57	-1.67	1.132
0.031	251.33	12.50	-1.74	1.139
0.015	252.44	12.44	-1.80	1.144

r_a/r_w = 2, l_{sc}/m = 0.2

K_o/K_a	Q	$2\pi s_w T/Q$	$\Delta W/2$	Q/Q_o
1	220.26	14.26	0	1
0.5	243.33	12.91	-1.35	1.105
0.25	259.14	12.12	-2.14	1.177
0.125	269.05	11.68	-2.58	1.222
0.062	274.71	11.43	-2.83	1.247
0.031	277.88	11.30	-2.96	1.262
0.020	279.23	11.25	-3.01	1.267
0.010	280.65	11.19	-3.07	1.274

118.

$r_a/r_w = 4$, $l_{sc}/m = 0.2$

K_o/K_a	Q	$2\pi Ts_w/Q$	$\Delta W/2$	Q/Q_o
1	217.48	14.45	0	1
0.5	262.67	11.96	-2.49	1.208
0.25	298.85	10.51	-3.94	1.374
0.125	323.98	9.70	-4.75	1.490
0.062	339.49	9.25	-5.20	1.561
0.031	348.46	9.02	-5.43	1.602
0.020	352.03	8.92	-5.53	1.619
0.010	355.38	8.84	-5.61	1.634

$r_a/r_w = 10$, $l_{sc}/m = 0.2$

K_o/K_a	Q	$2\pi s_w T/Q$	$\Delta W/2$	Q/Q_o
1	217.11	14.47	0	1
0.5	291.32	10.78	-3.69	1.342
0.25	365.80	8.59	-5.88	1.685
0.125	426.74	7.36	-7.11	1.966
0.062	468.43	6.71	-7.76	2.158
0.031	493.98	6.36	-8.11	2.275
0.02	503.86	6.24	-8.23	2.320
0.01	513.62	6.12	-8.35	2.366

$r_a/r_w = 28.6$, $l_{sc}/m = 0.2$

K_o/K_a	Q	$2\pi s_w T/Q$	$\Delta W/2$	Q/Q_o
1	216.82	14.48	0	1
0.5	310.52	10.12	-4.36	1.432
0.25	426.41	7.37	-7.11	1.967
0.125	544.33	5.77	-8.71	2.511
0.062	641.61	4.90	-9.58	2.959
0.031	709.32	4.43	-10.05	3.271
0.020	737.38	4.26	-10.22	3.401
0.010	763.32	4.12	-10.36	3.521

$r_a/r_w = 1.1$, $l_{sc}/m = 0.4$

K_o/K_a	Q	$2\pi Ts_w/Q$	$\Delta W/2$	Q/Q_o
1	318.48	9.86	0	1
0.5	322.00	9.76	-0.10	1.011
0.25	323.99	9.70	-0.16	1.017
0.125	324.99	9.67	-0.19	1.020
0.062	325.56	9.64	-0.22	1.022
0.031	326.22	9.63	-0.23	1.024
0.020	326.22	9.63	-0.23	1.024
0.010	326.22	9.63	-0.23	1.024

r_a/r_w = 1.2, l_{sc}/m = 0.4

K_o/K_a	Q	$2\pi T s_w/Q$	$\Delta W/2$	Q/Q_o
1	320.90	9.78	0	1
0.50	327.81	9.58	-0.20	1.022
0.25	331.86	9.47	-0.31	1.034
0.125	334.04	9.40	-0.38	1.041
0.062	335.48	9.36	-0.42	1.045
0.031	336.13	9.34	-0.44	1.047
0.020	336.13	9.34	-0.44	1.047
0.010	336.13	9.34	-0.44	1.047

r_a/r_w = 1.5, l_{sc}/m = 0.4

K_o/K_a	Q	$2\pi T s_w/Q$	$\Delta W/2$	Q/Q_o
1	313.44	10.02	0	1
0.50	328.12	9.57	-0.45	1.047
0.25	336.86	9.33	-0.69	1.075
0.125	340.81	9.22	-0.80	1.087
0.062	344.42	9.12	-0.90	1.099
0.031	345.87	9.08	-0.94	1.103
0.015	347.49	9.04	-0.98	1.109
0.007	348.65	9.01	-1.01	1.112

r_a/r_w = 2, l_{sc}/m = 0.4

K_o/K_a	Q	$2\pi T s_w/Q$	$\Delta W/2$	Q/Q_o
1	313.20	10.03	0	1
0.50	338.91	9.27	-0.76	1.082
0.25	355.15	8.85	-1.18	1.134
0.125	364.74	8.61	-1.42	1.165
0.062	369.84	8.49	-1.54	1.181
0.031	372.90	8.42	-1.61	1.191
0.020	374.13	8.40	-1.63	1.195
0.010	376.05	8.35	-1.68	1.201

r_a/r_w = 4, l_{sc}/m = 0.4

K_o/K_a	Q	$2\pi T s_w/Q$	$\Delta W/2$	Q/Q_o
1	311.30	10.09	0	1
0.50	363.11	8.65	-1.44	1.66
0.25	399.94	7.86	-2.23	1.285
0.125	423.50	7.42	-2.67	1.360
0.062	437.01	7.19	-2.90	1.404
0.031	444.77	7.06	-3.03	1.429
0.020	448.04	7.01	-3.08	1.439
0.010	451.28	6.96	-3.13	1.450

r_a/r_w = 10, l_{sc}/m = 0.4

K_o/K_a	Q	$2\pi\, s_w T/Q$	$\Delta W/2$	Q/Q_o
1	311.11	10.10	0	1
0.50	399.63	7.86	-2.24	1.285
0.25	474.85	6.62	-3.48	1.526
0.125	528.65	5.94	-4.16	1.699
0.062	562.10	5.59	-4.51	1.807
0.031	581.87	5.40	-4.70	1.870
0.020	589.54	5.33	-4.77	1.894
0.010	597.07	5.26	-4.84	1.919

r_a/r_w = 28.6, l_{sc}/m = 0.4

K_o/K_a	Q	$2\pi\, s_w T/Q$	$\Delta W/2$	Q/Q_o
1	311.00	10.10	0	1
0.50	434.47	7.23	-2.87	1.397
0.25	562.58	5.58	-4.52	1.809
0.125	670.49	4.69	-5.41	2.156
0.062	746.22	4.21	-5.89	2.399
0.031	793.74	3.96	-6.14	2.552
0.020	811.75	3.87	-6.23	2.610
0.010	824.77	3.81	-6.29	2.652

r_a/r_w = 1.1, l_{sc}/m = 0.6

K_o/K_a	Q	$2\pi\, s_w T/Q$	$\Delta W/2$	Q/Q_o
1	386.93	8.12	0	1
0.50	390.55	8.04	-0.08	1.009
0.25	392.51	8.00	-0.12	1.014
0.125	393.41	7.99	-0.13	1.017
0.062	394.02	7.95	-0.17	1.018
0.031	394.76	7.96	-0.18	1.020
0.020	394.76	7.96	-0.18	1.020
0.010	394.76	7.96	-0.18	1.020

r_a/r_w = 1.2, l_{sc}/m = 0.6

K_o/K_a	Q	$2\pi\, s_w T/Q$	$\Delta W/2$	Q/Q_o
1	388.60	8.08	0	1
0.50	395.58	7.94	-0.14	1.018
0.25	399.55	7.86	-0.22	1.028
0.125	401.61	7.82	-0.26	1.033
0.062	403.12	7.79	-0.29	1.037
0.031	403.69	7.78	-0.30	1.039
0.020	403.69	7.78	-0.30	1.039
0.010	403.69	7.78	-0.30	1.039

$r_a/r_w = 1.5$, $l_{sc}/m = 0.6$

K_O/K_a	Q	$2\pi\ Ts_w/Q$	$\Delta W/2$	Q/Q_o
1	383.32	8.20	0	1
0.50	398.49	7.88	-0.32	1.040
0.25	407.20	7.72	-0.48	1.062
0.125	412.00	7.63	-0.57	1.075
0.062	414.40	7.58	-0.62	1.081
0.031	415.93	7.55	-0.65	1.085
0.015	416.94	7.53	-0.67	1.087
0.007	419.60	7.49	-0.71	1.087

$r_a/r_w = 2$, $l_{sc}/m = 0.6$

K_O/K_a	Q	$2\pi\ s_w T/Q$	$\Delta W/2$	Q/Q_o
1	383.15	8.20	0	1
0.50	409.60	7.67	-0.53	1.069
0.25	425.55	7.38	-0.82	1.111
0.125	434.65	7.23	-0.97	1.134
0.062	439.20	7.15	-1.05	1.146
0.031	442.07	7.11	-1.09	1.154
0.020	443.28	7.09	-1.11	1.157
0.010	445.77	7.05	-1.15	1.163

$r_a/r_w = 4$, $l_{sc}/m = 0.6$

K_O/K_a	Q	$2\pi\ s_w T/Q$	$\Delta W/2$	Q/Q_o
1	381.64	8.23	0	1
0.50	435.49	7.21	-1.02	1.141
0.25	471.32	6.67	-1.56	1.235
0.125	493.20	6.37	-1.86	1.292
0.062	504.99	6.22	-2.01	1.323
0.031	511.81	6.14	-2.09	1.341
0.020	514.93	6.10	-2.13	1.349
0.010	518.15	6.06	-2.17	1.358

$r_a/r_w = 10$, $l_{sc}/m = 0.6$

K_O/K_a	Q	$2\pi\ s_w T/Q$	$\Delta W/2$	Q/Q_o
1	381.66	8.23	0	1
0.5	474.29	6.62	-1.61	1.243
0.25	545.98	5.75	-2.48	1.431
0.125	593.60	5.29	-2.94	1.555
0.062	621.52	5.05	-3.18	1.629
0.031	637.92	4.92	-3.31	1.671
0.020	644.39	4.88	-3.35	1.688
0.010	650.68	4.83	-3.40	1.705

$r_a/r_w = 28.6$, $l_{sc}/m = 0.6$

K_o/K_a	Q	$2\pi s_w T/Q$	$\Delta W/2$	Q/Q_o
1	381.70	8.23	0	1
0.5	517.09	6.08	-2.15	1.355
0.25	642.79	4.89	-3.34	1.684
0.125	738.22	4.26	-3.97	1.934
0.062	800.29	3.93	-4.30	2.097
0.031	837.97	3.75	-4.48	2.195
0.020	851.75	3.69	-4.54	2.231
0.010	857.01	3.67	-4.56	2.245

$r_a/r_w = 1.1$, $l_{sc}/m = 0.8$

K_o/K_a	Q	$2\pi T s_w/Q$	$\Delta W/2$	Q/Q_o
1	437.39	7.18	0	1
0.50	440.94	7.12	-0.06	1.008
0.25	442.85	7.09	-0.09	1.012
0.125	443.64	7.08	-0.10	1.014
0.062	444.00	7.07	-0.11	1.015
0.031	445.00	7.06	-0.12	1.017
0.020	445.56	7.05	-0.13	1.019
0.010	445.56	7.05	-0.13	1.019

$r_a/r_w = 1.2$, $l_{sc}/m = 0.8$

K_o/K_a	Q	$2\pi T s_w/Q$	$\Delta W/2$	Q/Q_o
1	438.34	7.17	0	1
0.50	445.07	7.06	-0.11	1.015
0.25	448.83	7.00	-0.17	1.024
0.125	450.68	6.97	-0.20	1.028
0.062	452.25	6.95	-0.22	1.031
0.031	452.77	6.94	-0.23	1.033
0.020	453.00	6.93	-0.24	1.033
0.010	453.00	6.93	-0.24	1.033

$r_a/r_w = 1.5$, $l_{sc}/m = 0.8$

K_o/K_a	Q	$2\pi T s_w/Q$	$\Delta W/2$	Q/Q_o
1	435.13	7.22	0	1
0.50	449.95	6.98	-0.24	1.034
0.25	458.22	6.86	-0.36	1.053
0.125	462.69	6.79	-0.43	1.063
0.062	464.58	6.76	-0.46	1.068
0.031	466.32	6.74	-0.48	1.072
0.020	467.36	6.72	-0.50	1.074
0.010	468.21	6.71	-0.51	1.076

$r_a/r_w = 2$, $l_{sc}/m = 0.8$

K_o/K_a	Q	$2\pi\, Ts_w/Q$	$\Delta W/2$	Q/Q_o
1	435.02	7.22	0	1
0.50	460.84	6.82	-0.40	1.059
0.25	475.86	6.60	-0.62	1.094
0.125	484.15	6.49	-0.73	1.113
0.062	487.97	6.44	-0.78	1.122
0.031	490.62	6.40	-0.82	1.128
0.020	491.74	6.39	-0.83	1.130
0.010	494.62	6.35	-0.87	1.137

$r_a/r_w = 4$, $l_{sc}/m = 0.8$

K_o/K_a	Q	$2\pi\, Ts_w/Q$	$\Delta W/2$	Q/Q_o
1	434.14	7.24	0	1
0.50	486.97	6.45	-0.79	1.122
0.25	520.47	6.04	-1.20	1.199
0.125	540.10	5.82	-1.42	1.244
0.062	549.94	5.71	-1.53	1.267
0.031	555.67	5.65	-1.59	1.280
0.020	558.65	5.62	-1.62	1.287
0.010	561.81	5.59	-1.65	1.294

$r_a/r_w = 10$, $l_{sc}/m = 0.8$

K_o/K_a	Q	$2\pi\, s_w T/Q$	$\Delta W/2$	Q/Q_o
1	434.17	7.24	0	1
0.50	525.88	5.97	-1.27	1.211
0.25	592.10	5.31	-1.93	1.364
0.125	633.50	4.96	-2.28	1.459
0.062	656.37	4.79	-2.45	1.512
0.031	669.93	4.69	-2.55	1.543
0.020	675.32	4.65	-2.59	1.555
0.010	680.59	4.62	-2.62	1.568

$r_a/r_w = 28.6$, $l_{sc}/m = 0.8$

K_o/K_a	Q	$2\pi\, s_w T/Q$	$\Delta W/2$	Q/Q_o
1	434.35	7.24	0	1
0.5	574.01	5.47	-1.77	1.322
0.25	693.56	4.53	-2.71	1.597
0.125	777.88	4.04	-3.20	1.791
0.062	830.01	3.79	-3.45	1.911
0.031	861.32	3.65	-3.59	1.983
0.020	872.22	3.60	-3.64	2.008
0.010	872.80	3.60	-3.64	2.009

Appendix IV

Tabulation of Results for Transient Flow
with Permeability Improvement in the
Inner Zone.

IV-1 Fully Penetrating Wells

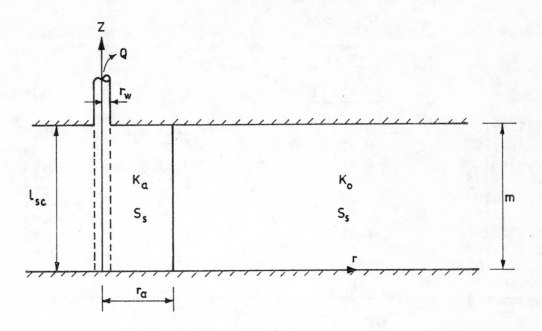

For all finite element results obtained

$m = 50, \ r_W = 1, \ Q = 100, \ K_O = 0.1, \ S_S = 0.1 \times 10^{-4}$

Table 18 : Results for transient flow towards fully penetrating wells pumped at constant discharge.

The results listed in this table are plotted in Fig . 50.
These results were obtained by using a two-dimensional mesh similar to mesh 2a in Fig. 8   but with the external radius $r_o = 5000$.

$$l_{sc}/m = 1, \quad r_a/r_w = 10$$

$$K_o/K_a = 0.50$$

Early time results

$1/u_w$	$(W + \Delta W)/2$	$W/2$	$\Delta W/2$
0.134×10	0.33	0.51	-0.18
0.268×10	0.43	0.67	-0.24
0.536×10	0.54	0.87	-0.33
0.107×10^2	0.68	1.10	-0.42
0.214×10^2	0.82	1.36	-0.54
0.429×10^2	0.98	1.65	-0.67
0.858×10^2	1.15	1.95	-0.80
0.172×10^3	1.35	2.27	-0.92
0.343×10^3	1.59	2.60	-1.01
0.686×10^3	1.87	2.94	-1.07
0.137×10^4	2.17	3.28	-1.11

Late time results

$1/u_w$	$(W + \Delta W)/2$	$W/2$	$\Delta W/2$
0.275×10^4	2.50	3.63	-1.13
0.549×10^4	2.83	3.97	-1.14
0.110×10^5	3.17	4.32	-1.15
0.220×10^5	3.51	4.66	-1.15
0.439×10^5	3.85	5.00	-1.15
0.879×10^5	4.20	5.35	-1.15
0.175×10^6	4.55	5.70	-1.15
0.352×10^6	4.89	6.05	-1.16
0.703×10^6	5.24	6.39	-1.15
0.141×10^7	5.59	6.73	-1.16
0.281×10^7	5.93	7.08	-1.15
0.562×10^7	6.28	7.43	-1.15

$\Delta W/2$ for corresponding steady flow case = -1.14

$$l_{sc}/m = 1, \quad r_a/r_w = 10$$

$$K_o/K_a = 0.25$$

Early time results

$1/u_w$	$(W+ \Delta W)/2$	$W/2$	$\Delta W/2$
0.134×10	0.21	0.51	-0.30
0.268×10	0.27	0.67	-0.40
0.536×10	0.33	0.87	-0.54
0.107×10^2	0.40	1.10	-0.70
0.214×10^2	0.48	1.36	-0.88
0.429×10^2	0.58	1.65	-1.07
0.858×10^2	0.70	1.95	-1.25
0.172×10^3	0.86	2.27	-1.41
0.343×10^3	1.07	2.60	-1.53
0.686×10^3	1.32	2.94	-1.62
0.137×10^4	1.61	3.28	-1.67

Late time results

$1/u_w$	$(W+ \Delta W)/2$	$W/2$	$\Delta W/2$
0.275×10^4	1.93	3.63	-1.70
0.549×10^4	2.26	3.97	-1.71
0.110×10^5	2.60	4.32	-1.72
0.220×10^5	2.94	4.66	-1.73
0.439×10^5	3.28	5.00	-1.72
0.879×10^5	3.63	5.35	-1.72
0.175×10^6	3.97	5.70	-1.73
0.352×10^6	4.31	6.05	-1.74
0.703×10^6	4.67	6.39	-1.72
0.141×10^7	5.01	6.73	-1.72
0.281×10^7	5.35	7.08	-1.73
0.562×10^7	5.70	7.43	-1.73

$\Delta W/2$ for corresponding steady flow case = -1.71

$$l_{sc}/m = 1, \quad r_a/r_w = 10$$

$$K_o/K_a = 0.125$$

Early time results

$1/u_w$	$(W+ \Delta W)/2$	$W/2$	$\Delta W/2$
0.134×10	0.12	0.51	-0.39
0.268×10	0.16	0.67	-0.51
0.536×10	0.19	0.87	-0.68
0.107×10^2	0.23	1.10	-0.87
0.214×10^2	0.28	1.36	-1.08
0.429×10^2	0.35	1.65	-1.30
0.858×10^2	0.46	1.95	-1.49
0.172×10^3	0.61	2.27	-1.66
0.343×10^3	0.81	2.60	-1.79
0.686×10^3	1.05	2.94	-1.89
0.137×10^4	1.34	3.28	-1.94

Late Time Results

$1/u_W$	$(W+ \Delta W)/2$	$W/2$	$\Delta W/2$
0.275×10^4	1.65	3.63	-1.98
0.549×10^4	1.97	3.97	-2.00
0.110×10^5	2.31	4.32	-2.01
0.220×10^5	2.65	4.66	-2.01
0.439×10^5	3.00	5.00	-2.00
0.879×10^5	3.33	5.35	-2.02
0.175×10^6	3.68	5.70	-2.02
0.352×10^6	4.03	6.05	-2.02
0.703×10^6	4.39	6.39	-2.00
0.141×10^7	4.72	6.73	-2.01
0.281×10^7	5.07	7.08	-2.01
0.562×10^7	5.42	7.43	-2.01

$W/2$ for corresponding steady flow case = -1.99

$l_{sc}/m = 1$, $r_a/r_w = 10$

$K_o/K_a = 0.031$

Early time results

$1/u_W$	$(W+ \Delta W)/2$	$W/2$	$\Delta W/2$
0.134×10	0.04	0.51	-0.47
0.268×10	0.05	0.67	-0.62
0.536×10	0.06	0.87	-0.81
0.107×10^2	0.08	1.10	-1.02
0.214×10^2	0.11	1.36	-1.25
0.429×10^2	0.18	1.65	-1.47
0.858×10^2	0.27	1.95	-1.68
0.172×10^3	0.41	2.27	-1.86
0.343×10^3	0.61	2.60	-1.99
0.686×10^3	0.85	2.94	-2.09
0.137×10^4	1.12	3.28	-2.16

Late time results

$1/u_W$	$(W+ \Delta W)/2$	$W/2$	$\Delta W/2$
0.275×10^4	1.43	3.63	-2.20
0.549×10^4	1.75	3.97	-2.22
0.110×10^5	2.10	4.32	-2.22
0.220×10^5	2.42	4.66	-2.24
0.439×10^5	2.75	5.00	-2.25
0.879×10^5	3.10	5.35	-2.25
0.175×10^6	3.47	5.70	-2.23
0.352×10^6	3.76	6.05	-2.29
0.703×10^6	4.11	6.39	-2.28
0.141×10^7	4.48	6.73	-2.25
0.281×10^7	4.84	7.08	-2.24
0.562×10^7	5.11	7.43	-2.32

$\Delta W/2$ for corresponding steady flow case = -2.20

IV-2 Partially Penetrating Wells

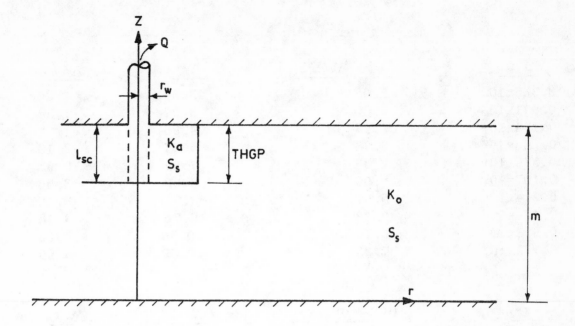

For all finite element results obtained $m = 50$, $r_w = 1$,
THGP = l_{sc}, $Q = 100$, $K_O = 0.1$, $S_S = 0.1 \times 10^{-4}$.

Table 19 : Results for transient flow towards partially penetrating wells pumped at constant discharge.

The results listed in this table are plotted in Fig. 50

$$l_{sc}/m = 0.2, \quad r_a/r_w = 10$$
$$K_o/K_a = 0.5$$

Early time results

$1/u_w$	$(W + \Delta W)/2$	$W/2$	$\Delta W/2$
0.335×10	2.05	3.05	-1.00
0.671×10	2.60	3.97	-1.37
0.134×10^2	3.18	4.95	-1.77
0.268×10^2	3.78	5.97	-2.19
0.536×10^2	4.39	7.02	-2.63
0.107×10^3	5.00	8.00	-3.00
0.214×10^3	5.61	8.91	-3.30
0.429×10^3	6.22	9.70	-3.48
0.858×10^3	6.76	10.36	-3.60
0.172×10^4	7.23	10.89	-3.66

Late time results

$1/u_w$	$(W + \Delta W)/2$	$W/2$	$\Delta W/2$
0.268×10^4	7.45	11.15	-3.70
0.536×10^4	7.81	11.53	-3.72
0.107×10^5	8.18	11.88	-3.70
0.215×10^5	8.57	12.22	-3.65
0.429×10^5	8.85	12.56	-3.71
0.858×10^5	9.25	12.90	-3.65
0.172×10^6	9.54	13.22	-3.68
0.343×10^6	9.95	13.56	-3.61
0.687×10^6	10.22	13.97	-3.75
0.137×10^7	10.62	14.26	-3.64
0.275×10^7	10.92	14.66	-3.74

$\Delta W/2$ for corresponding steady flow case = -3.69.

$$l_{sc}/m = 0.2, \quad r_a/r_w = 10$$
$$K_o/K_a = 0.25$$

Early time results

$1/u_w$	$(W + \Delta W)/2$	$W/2$	$\Delta W/2$
0.335×10	1.32	3.05	-1.73
0.671×10	1.64	3.97	-2.33
0.134×10^2	1.97	4.95	-2.98
0.268×10^2	2.30	5.97	-3.67
0.536×10^2	2.67	7.02	-4.35
0.107×10^3	3.10	8.00	-4.90

0.214×10^3	3.59	8.91	-5.32
0.429×10^3	4.10	9.70	-5.60
0.858×10^3	4.61	10.36	-5.75
0.172×10^4	5.05	10.89	-5.84

Late time results

$1/u_W$	$(W + \Delta W)/2$	$W/2$	$\Delta W/2$
0.268×10^4	5.30	11.15	-5.85
0.536×10^4	5.67	11.53	-5.86
0.107×10^5	6.02	11.88	-5.86
0.215×10^5	6.33	12.22	-5.89
0.429×10^5	6.68	12.56	-5.88
0.858×10^5	7.02	12.90	-5.88
0.172×10^6	7.36	13.22	-5.86
0.343×10^6	7.70	13.56	-5.86
0.687×10^6	8.04	13.97	-5.93
0.137×10^7	8.39	14.26	-5.87
0.275×10^7	8.73	14.66	-5.93

$\Delta W/2$ for corresponding steady flow case = -5.88

$$l_{sc}/m = 0.2, \quad r_a/r_W = 10$$

$$K_o/K_a = 0.125$$

Early time results

$1/u_W$	$(W + \Delta W)/2$	$W/2$	$\Delta W/2$
0.335×10	0.82	3.05	-2.23
0.671×10	1.00	3.97	-2.97
0.134×10^2	1.18	4.95	-3.77
0.268×10^2	1.39	5.97	-4.58
0.536×10^2	1.66	7.02	-5.36
0.107×10^3	2.00	8.00	-6.00
0.214×10^3	2.44	8.91	-6.47
0.429×10^3	2.93	9.70	-6.77
0.858×10^3	3.40	10.36	-6.96
0.172×10^4	3.83	10.89	-7.06

Late time results

$1/u_W$	$(W + \Delta W)/2$	$W/2$	$\Delta W/2$
0.268×10^4	4.09	11.15	-7.06
0.536×10^4	4.45	11.53	-7.08
0.107×10^5	4.79	11.88	-7.09
0.215×10^5	5.12	12.22	-7.10
0.429×10^5	5.45	12.56	-7.11
0.858×10^5	5.79	12.90	-7.11
0.172×10^6	6.13	13.22	-7.09
0.343×10^6	6.47	13.56	-7.09
0.687×10^6	6.82	13.97	-7.15
0.137×10^7	7.16	14.26	-7.10
0.275×10^7	7.50	14.66	-7.16

$\Delta W/2$ for corresponding steady flow case = -7.11

$$l_{sc}/m = 0.2, \quad r_a/r_w = 10$$

$$K_o/K_a = 0.031$$

Early time results

$1/u_w$	$(W + \Delta W)/2$	$W/2$	$\Delta W/2$
0.335×10	0.30	3.05	-2.75
0.671×10	0.36	3.97	-3.61
0.134×10^2	0.45	4.95	-4.50
0.268×10^2	0.59	5.97	-5.38
0.536×10^2	0.81	7.02	-6.21
0.107×10^3	1.12	8.00	-6.88
0.214×10^3	1.51	8.91	-7.40
0.429×10^3	1.97	9.70	-7.73
0.858×10^3	2.47	10.36	-7.89
0.172×10^4	2.85	10.89	-8.04

Late time results

$1/u_w$	$(W + \Delta W)/2$	$W/2$	$\Delta W/2$
0.268×10^4	3.08	11.15	-8.07
0.536×10^4	3.43	11.53	-8.10
0.107×10^5	3.79	11.88	-8.09
0.215×10^5	4.12	12.22	-8.10
0.429×10^5	4.46	12.56	-8.10
0.858×10^5	4.77	12.90	-8.13

$\Delta W/2$ for corresponding steady flow case = -8.10.